CHRISTIANITY AND CULTURE
IN THE CROSSFIRE

Christianity and Culture in the Crossfire

Edited by

David A. Hoekema *and* Bobby Fong

CALVIN CENTER FOR CHRISTIAN SCHOLARSHIP
GRAND RAPIDS, MICHIGAN

WILLIAM B. EERDMANS PUBLISHING COMPANY
GRAND RAPIDS, MICHIGAN / CAMBRIDGE, U.K.

Published jointly 1997 by the Calvin Center for Christian Scholarship and
Wm. B. Eerdmans Publishing Co.
255 Jefferson Ave. S.E., Grand Rapids, Michigan 49503 /
P.O. Box 163, Cambridge CB3 9PU U.K.

02 01 00 99 98 97   7 6 5 4 3 2 1

Library of Congress Cataloging-in-Publication Data

Christianity and culture in the crossfire / edited by
David A. Hoekema and Bobby Fong.
Includes bibliographical references.
p.   cm.
ISBN 0-8028-4323-9 (pbk.: alk. paper)
1. Christianity and culture. 2. Christianity and culture —
United States. 3. Multiculturalism — Religious aspects — Christianity.
4. Postmodernism — Religious aspects — Christianity.
5. Feminism — Religious aspects — Christianity.
I. Hoekema, David A. II. Fong, Bobby.
BR115.C8C445   1997
261 — dc21   97-4924
                                    CIP

The essay by Miroslav Volf is adapted from a chapter in his recent book *Exclusion and Embrace: A Theological Exploration of Identity, Otherness, and Reconciliation* (Abingdon Press, 1996), and is reprinted by kind permission of Abingdon Press.

This collection is
dedicated to the memory of
Jean Hampton,
whose death while the volume was in preparation
cut short a distinguished career
in moral and political philosophy
and took from us a valued colleague,
friend, and sister in the family of God.

Contents

CONTENTS

II. Feminism and the Possibility of Objectivity

III. Postmodernism and the Standing of Religious Belief

IV. Strangers, Friends, and New Communities

Foreword

THIS BOOK IS a product of the Calvin Center for Christian Scholarship (CCCS), which was established at Calvin College in 1976. The purpose of the CCCS is to promote creative, articulate, and rigorous Christian scholarship that addresses important theoretical and practical issues.

The present volume is the result of the inspiration and effort of David Hoekema and Bobby Fong. They conceived of the idea of bringing topflight scholars together to allow frank discussion and to enable fresh perspectives to be articulated on the whole matter of "culture wars." They were awarded a grant from the CCCS, and in due course a conference was held here at Calvin College.

Those of us who helped organize the conference believe it to have been one of the more exciting academic meetings we have attended. There were great expectations of good interchange and new departures. We were not disappointed. The chapters in this book are the measured, revised thoughts of the presenters, who, upon reflection on the conference dialogue, have transformed their spoken papers into literary essays. This collection is not a mere reproduction of conference papers in symposium form, but a set of essays self-consciously written, edited, and arranged to allow discussion to go forward. David Hoekema has written a good introduction to these essays, so there is no need for me to repeat it. I echo his hope that the book will help in the Christian plea for peace in the "culture wars."

Ronald A. Wells

DAVID A. HOEKEMA

INTRODUCTION

Christianity and Culture in the Crossfire

WHY COME TOGETHER to discuss Christianity and culture? For immediate reasons one need only listen to the news. Recently the Supreme
Court heard oral arguments defending the appropriateness of displaying
a cross in a downtown plaza, in a location where permission had already
been granted for seasonal display of a menorah and a Christmas tree.

A familiar story, you may think. But there is something unusual
about this case. The request to display a cross came not from a church
but from a private nonprofit group, and not from one whose name
springs to mind when we enumerate the laborers in the Lord's vineyard:
it came from the Ku Klux Klan. The grand cyclops of the Klan told a
National Public Radio reporter that one of his organization's goals is
to remind unbelievers of the sacrificial death of Jesus Christ. A lawyer
representing the Klan acknowledged to the reporter that, if his client's
group were to come to power in the United States, they would probably
seek to deport him along with all other Jews. Where, in this perplexing
political and religious muddle, is the side of Christianity, and is it in
harmony with or in opposition to culture?

The examples proliferate. Some Christians demand legislative permission for school prayer, while others believe it would transgress
constitutional limits and cheapen religion. Politicians invoke biblical
standards of responsibility in the family in calling for abandonment of

[1]

the welfare system, while bishops build a vigorous defense of aid to the poor on the same Bible. Outside prisons where executions are scheduled, church members carry placards decrying leniency toward criminals and citing the Mosaic *lex talionis*. Facing them across the police barricades are fellow church members who denounce the death penalty as an unnecessary and unjustified exercise in state-sanctioned violence that does not bring justice but only satisfies the desire for revenge.

More central to our topic is the face-off over the barricades of academia which has been labeled a culture war. The partisans on one side are the heirs of those great iconoclasts of the previous century — Marx, Freud, and Nietzsche — whose broadly parallel critiques of conventional economics, psychology, and moral philosophy unmasked the smug self-deception with which Western thinkers had long reassured themselves that their parochial viewpoint was that of a pure rationality transcending history and community. In distinct but related ways, the advocates of feminism, postmodernism, and multiculturalism have argued that such transcendental rationality is an illusion, a goal that cannot even be coherently described, let alone achieved. Knowledge, they urge, is always situated in a person, in a time, in a community. We are not rational, fact-verifying devices: we are human persons, male and female persons, African American and Asian American and European American persons. Our questions no less than our answers are situated in our concreteness. Both are products of a dynamic process in which our minds do not snap photographs of the world but rather converse with it. As our search for answers leads us on, both the knower and the known, both we and our world, experience profound changes.

From the three forebears already mentioned, many feminist and postmodernist theorists have inherited a deep distrust of all religious belief. Belief in a transcendent creator and sustainer, said Marx, is a narcotic that serves to paralyze political will. It is a projection of unsatisfiable wishes, explained Freud. It is an expression of the resentment of the weak against the strong, added Nietzsche, and he summed up the joint diagnosis of these three clinical metaphysicians: God is dead. Many theorists who follow in the footsteps of these three giants are so convinced of the accuracy of the diagnosis that they scarcely bother to examine the vast and pervasive human religious enterprise to see whether God may still be breathing.

Small wonder, then, that the leaders of the opposing party in the culture wars have rallied to the defense of both the God of the Bible and the ideal of objective and impartial knowledge — both of these being objects of devotion, in a manner of speaking, for the piety that is decried by postmodernist iconoclasts. The defensive forces construe the attack on impersonal and objective reason as an attack on all that is good, true, or beautiful. Feminism and postmodernism, it is said, are advance parties for a nihilistic relativism in which all ideas and all values are equally valid, in which truth has vanished and morality has yielded the field to gratification. At its rawest, this counterattack is heard in the rantings of talk-show hosts who claim to uphold Christian values against "feminazis" and intolerant enforcers of political correctness. More sophisticated versions are sounded by eminent Christian scholars who urge their colleagues not to surrender the ramparts of disinterested and impersonal rationality as the touchstone of responsible scholarship and of knowledge itself, since Christian faith and practice must surely collapse if that ideal is abandoned.

The cultural war between these perspectives has often been heated. Why venture into the zone where charges and countercharges are flying? Because it is our conviction — I speak first of all for co-organizer Bobby Fong and myself, but also for many colleagues — that each side has misunderstood and misconstrued the other. The conflict between post-modernism and multiculturalism on the one side, and Christian belief on the other, has been waged along the wrong lines of battle. Troops have been massed in defense of positions that have no strategic importance, while possibilities for negotiation and mutually beneficial settlement have repeatedly been spurned.

This predilection for war over peace talks is unfortunate in two ways. On the one hand, the relative silence of thoughtful Christian voices in the debate has impoverished national discussion of these matters. A tradition that has profoundly influenced the current state of American intellectual culture, and within which questions of truth and justice have been vigorously debated for two millennia, has too often been ignored, or reduced to irresponsible oversimplifications, by the officers leading the cultural battle on both sides. On the other hand, even where recent writings about community, gender, and the social bases of knowledge have direct bearing on issues of Christian faith and practice, leaders in the Christian community have given them too little consideration or dismissed them without serious examination.

[3]

The purpose of this collection, as of the conference at which earlier versions of these essays were presented to a large and diverse audience, is to persuade both Christian and secular observers to take a more nuanced view of the issues under discussion — to see that, although some elements of emerging theories of knowledge and reality are in conflict with Christian construals of knowledge and the world, other elements are much-needed correctives to the uncritical orthodoxies that dominate modern religious as well as secular thought.

To that end, eleven prominent scholars, representing the perspectives of philosophy, theology, history, and the sciences, have contributed essays in which they address questions such as the following:

Is there a "culture war" being waged in the academy today and, if so, who are the warring parties?

What fundamental commitments concerning the nature and source of knowledge and the relationship between knowledge and the world underlie the feminist and postmodernist critique of Enlightenment models?

In what respects is this critique, initially directed against prevailing secular theories and methodologies, equally telling when applied to the positions typical of Christian thinkers? In what respects are these critical movements aligned with, and not opposed to, Christianity?

Is knowledge generated by a community, not simply by an individual? Do communitarian moral values demand a communitarian theory of knowledge?

Is there in Christian social thought and practice a communitarian perspective that is less liable to lapse into authoritarianism or fascism than are its secular counterparts?

What place do race and ethnicity have in a community shaped by Christian values? In what ways is Christianity complicit with structures of exclusion and racism, and what resources can it deploy to overcome them?

The essays in the collection were originally presented at an interdisciplinary conference held at Calvin College in April 1995, under the sponsorship of the Calvin Center for Christian Scholarship. Each contributor had a chance to read and discuss the other ten essays at the conference, to engage the other contributors in dialogue both in formal panel discussions and in informal settings, and to revise his or her essay in response to this exchange. We believe the resulting collection offers as rich an array of thoughtful and articulate voices, most but not all from within various Christian intellectual communities, as can be found anywhere to assist lay church members, members of the clergy, and those involved in higher education in understanding the significance and implications of the cultural developments we have mentioned for Christian faith today.

As we welcome these contemporary voices, we must acknowledge our debt to a preeminent Christian scholar of a previous generation. Two score and five years have passed since the publication of a book that set the stage for our conversation: H. Richard Niebuhr's landmark study of *Christ and Culture*. In that study Niebuhr drew a fivefold distinction between the strands in the Christian tradition that set Christ and culture in intractable opposition, that accommodate Christ to culture, that posit a synthesis of Christian and cultural values, that hold the two in essential paradox, and that look for a transformation or conversion of culture by Christ. Niebuhr's eloquent defense of the last of these five options, which he traces from the Gospel of John through Augustine to Calvin and his successors, has been a powerful recruiting tool for Reformed theology, which Niebuhr presents in its most inclusive and attractive light. One wishes that more of Calvin's heirs shared Niebuhr's ability to limn the outlines of Reformed theology in ways that highlight its beauty and grandeur, leaving aside polemic but aiming instead to weave together valuable strands from other Christian traditions.

Niebuhr was well aware of how easily the Reformed affirmation of culture under the rule of Christ may slip into something quite different, and he made this trenchant observation of the American legacy of one of the greatest philosophical minds of the Reformed tradition:

> Jonathan Edwards, with his sensitive and profound views of creation, sin, and justification, with his understanding of the way of conversion and his millennial hopes, became in America the founder of a movement of thought about Christ as the regenerator of man in his culture. It has never wholly lost momentum, though it is often perverted into banal, Pelagian theurgisms in which men were concerned with the

symptoms of sin, not its roots, and thought it possible to channel the grace and power of God into the canals they engineered. Thus the conversionism of Edwards was used to justify the psychological mechanics of a shabby revivalism, with its mass production of renovated souls, and the sociological science of that part of the social gospel which expected to change prodigal mankind by improving the quality of the husks served in the pigsty.[1]

I will not attempt to distinguish all of the targets against which Niebuhr aims his barbs in this paragraph. But it is evident that they are by no means absent from the church today, nor have the Reformed churches identified any theological vaccine that protects against such infections. (I choose my metaphor with deliberately ironic intent, since Edwards's death early in his term as president of Princeton University resulted from the live cowpox vaccine against smallpox that he required all faculty members to receive. Biology, like theology, can take an unexpected and unwelcome course in its growth and development.) The vision of Christ as the one who redeems and transforms every dimension of human endeavor, of God drawing all things natural and man-made unto God's self through the life and the sacrificial death of the Son, shines powerfully through the half-century since Niebuhr's book was published, providing a background to our discussions in this collection.

We have organized the essays into four sections. The first contains four rather diverse reflections on the theology of culture, particularly the relationship between cultural practices and the values and traditions in which they are grounded. In the essay which opens the collection, church historian Martin Marty reviews the great multiplicity of cultures present in the American scene and traces their emergence to needs unfilled by modern social structures. "It is significant that Christian people are in every one of these subcultures that make up multicultures," he writes — "that is why I am never able to see the 'culture wars' on binary, bifocal, bivocal, polarized, God versus Satan, Christ versus Antichrist, we versus they terms." In response, we are called to study these cultures through the lens of the humanities; to engage in politics, and

1. H. Richard Niebuhr, *Christ and Culture* (New York: HarperCollins, 1951), pp. 219-20.

particularly in community building; to accept the necessity of working in a "profane" world; and to participate in a variety of modes of existence.

Miroslav Volf, a Croatian theologian now teaching in the United States, presses the issues of culture and theology to a deeper level in his meditation on truth, freedom, and violence. His essay opens by recalling the toast of Winston Smith in Orwell's *Nineteen Eighty-Four:* "To the past," to which another character rejoins that "who controls the past, controls the future." Elie Wiesel similarly insists upon memory as the key to knowing ourselves and our future, Volf notes. Indeed, the central Christian practice of eucharistic celebration is an exercise in remembering. But memory can play us false. In the middle section of the essay Volf develops an imagined objection from a member of his audience, challenging the claim that we can know the past. Volf answers the objection in a concluding discussion of the relationship between truth and power, as illuminated by postmodernist theories of truth and as exemplified in Jesus' dialogue with Pilate in John's Gospel.[2]

The way in which the past shapes the present in the Christian tradition can be better understood by exploring parallel aspects of the Jewish roots from which it sprang. In the next essay, Jewish theologian and historian Jacob Neusner presents an argument that the transcendent reference of Judaism as a religion has been transmuted in contemporary societies into a secular focus on the nation of Israel. From a theological standpoint, ethnicity and race do not exist. The growing emphasis in multiculturalism on ethnic identity has gone hand in hand with the eclipse of religious commitment and the triumph of secularism. And once one has gone down this path, to return is extremely difficult, for "the alternative to secularism is not religion, it is nihilism." Neusner closes with a call to reaffirm the uniqueness of "holy books," which "record and preserve what it means to know God — as much as the dance records and preserves what it means to embody music."

Closing this section on theologies and cultures is Peter Paris's reflection as an African American theologian on the way in which the struggle for racial justice in the United States "represents two opposing world-

---

2. This essay, the only one in the present collection that will also appear elsewhere, is part of a chapter in Volf's forthcoming study *Exclusion and Embrace: A Theological Exploration of Identity, Otherness, and Reconciliation.*

views": the persistent doctrine of racial inequality that was deeply infused into the history of the European presence in the New World, and the emerging possibility of "a new moral order" in which all nations and peoples will be embraced in a spirit of pluralism. Recent celebrations of "the Columbus myth" have revealed the power of racist ideology over contemporary political thought. In dialogue with African and Native American philosophical and theological traditions, however, European culture may yet come to embrace a vision of equality and mutual affirmation.

The second section of the collection brings together three essays that are very diverse in their grounding and their goals but share a focus on the challenge of feminist scholarship to the academy today, all of them contributed by philosophers whose work is held in high esteem in their disciplinary communities. Nicholas Wolterstorff examines the perspectival claims to knowledge that are put forward by emerging scholarship in feminist epistemology, Native American history, gay literary studies, and liberation theology. These movements reject the "Grand Project" of Western philosophy, the quest for a unified theory of objective truth, which runs from Plato through contemporary analytic philosophy. The critics help us see what that tradition has denied: that each of us engages in the search for truth not as an ideally rational inquirer but as a particular person, with both "hard-wired" and "programmed" capacities and sensitivities. "Certain of the perspectives which belong to our narrative identities," he suggests, may give us access to "realms of reality" otherwise closed to us.

Elizabeth Minnich contributes a more personal exploration of the relationship between feminist philosophy and religious vision. She describes the way in which, in her upbringing, the search for truth was inextricably bound up with the struggle for justice, the latter ideal being framed in political and not religious terms. In reflecting on the source and nature of the "deep questions" that religion seeks to answer, she is led to reflect on "how all faiths, including 'faith' in reason, have been expressed in human constructs that have historically contradicted their own highest aspirations." The collapse of the dream that reason alone can banish all injustice should provide the needed cue for "both politics and religion (the two areas most notably banned from the secular ivory tower)" to "move forward to take up [these] hard and important questions."

Jean Hampton's essay, both philosophical and practical in its intent and methods, focuses on the conduct of inquiry among feminist philosophers and their antagonists. Decrying the hasty dismissal and unsympathetic reading that have been too common in these debates, Hampton offers advice on "how to fight." Our disagreements need to be worked out in a spirit of mutual respect, she urges — and this duty should be even more readily recognized by Christians than by those who admit no values except human desires. Equally important, notwithstanding all the criticism that feminists have directed against traditional canons of rationality, our disputes must be conducted on the basis of reasoned argument, for only in this way does one genuinely honor and respect the opponent. Jean's tragic death during the period when this collection was in preparation has taken from among us a voice of rare clarity and a person of unusual integrity, to whose memory we have dedicated this volume.

The next two essays share a focus on the postmodernist movement — if indeed viewpoints so varied in their perspective and so stubbornly resistant to generalization can be classified as a movement. Literary scholar Wayne Booth traces the way in which postmodernism has provided "a resurrection of humane rhetoric" in response to the sterility of positivism. We may define religion, provisionally, as a worldview that acknowledges brokenness in the world and in our human selves, that offers a narrative of how the world came to be and of our place in it, and that calls us to obedience "not just to others but to the Other." By this account, deconstruction, as exemplified in the recent writing of Jacques Derrida, is deeply religious in its methods and its goals, for it seeks to restore a sense that human lives matter profoundly. Derrida, he suggests, is "a theologian in disguise," despite his denial that we can speak meaningfully of God.

In his account of the relationship between Christianity and postmodernism, Mark Schwehn opens with a vivid image — the geometry of Thomas Jefferson's design of the Rotunda at Charlottesville — to illustrate the continual tension between Enlightenment and tradition. The many voices raised in dissent against Enlightenment ideals, Schwehn suggests, are not a coherent movement but a set of loosely related voices, not really rejecting modernity but attempting to reformulate it. Wolterstorff advises wisely that postmodern perspectives may lend access to new realms of reality, Schwehn argues, yet we must not forget that new perspectives may also trick the eye. A grounding in tradition and community is necessary to help form our judgment, and the path that will lead us to truth is not that of disinterested rationality but that of obedience. Directing the hermeneutics of suspicion within the Christian community as well as outward, we should come "on the one hand to suspect the exclusivist claims of Christianity and on the other hand to trust the unfathomable dimensions of God's love and mercy."

In the last section of the collection are two essays that undertake to respond to many of the ideas presented by the others, more than to mark out new territory of their own. Paula Brownlee, a chemist now serving as president of a major higher education association, writes candidly of her sense of alienation from the mode of discourse of the humanities disciplines. There is a similar separation between her life as a church member and her life as a scientist. Citing Jean Hampton's reflections on how to conduct our disagreements, she observes that between the realm of science and the realm of religion silence is more common than open debate. "We need to recognize first the many boundaries of disciplines and of religious belief which make us profoundly strangers to each other," she observes — and then we will see that "the metaphor of welcoming the stranger represents a strong vision of what higher education and liberal learning should be about."

Dennis O'Brien's closing essay ties together many themes of the preceding reflections with specific reference to the crisis of authority in Catholic higher education. Ever since Descartes, the academy has rejected any appeal to authority as a ground of truth. The ideal of purely rational inquiry has proven insufficient to arrive at any truth, but the evanescent "shape-shifter" self of postmodernism is equally inadequate from the standpoint of the believing community. Citing Walker Percy and Henry James, O'Brien suggests that "the biblical story" is neither a source of spiritual insight nor a body of facts, but rather a "germ," like the narrative core of a novel — "a set of revelatory conditions and circumstances with which humans write out the story of life."

We may ask once again, before turning to the essays themselves: Is it helpful to entertain the image of Christianity and culture in the crossfire? Some would place Christianity today in the cross hairs, the target at which its cultured despisers aim their scorn, the antiquated system of superstition whose hold on the human heart they aspire to destroy. Others might suggest that as Christians we stand at a crossroads, a parting of the way between faithfulness to orthodoxy and capitulation to relativism.

But let us hold to the image of the crossfire. We stand on dangerous and disputed ground, ever liable to attack from either side. Yet we stand together, and we seek to draw each side out from behind its sandbags, up out of its trenches, to sit down with us and explore the possibility of deeper understanding and deeper insights. We call for a cease-fire and for a peace parley. But the enterprise has its hazards. On too many fields of conflict, peacekeepers become targets. We hope that the reflections here offered will open channels of more fruitful communication between Christians and their sometime antagonists and suggest possibilities, not for firing and crossfire, but rather for cross-fertilization, with its attendant promise of more abundant and more delicious fruit.

PART ONE

Cultures and the Theologies
on Which They Stand

MARTIN E. MARTY

Cross-Multicultures in the Crossfire:
The Humanities and Political Interests

I. The Situation

"Christianity," in the dictionary sense of the term, cannot be endangered in the crossfire, because it could not be hit. "Christianity" is vaporous, evanescent, residual, abstract, a construct representing what is left after the church has moved on. In the present context, then, it is a code word for "Christian people," their institutions and texts and creations, which are indeed vulnerable to crossfiring.

Christianity comes to us in many forms; there are almost twenty-five thousand denominations. Since these are all divided down the middle in near schisms, we begin with fifty thousand entities. Yet most particularities do not even follow denominational lines. It is easy therefore to think of multi-Christianity.

"Culture," the second noun of the conference title, cannot easily be defined, but it can be pointed to. Here let it represent everything that humans do to and make of nature. Since humans work in concert, band together, come as families and clans and tribes and nations, they also merit consideration in "multi's," as in multicultures.

"The" implies a particular and single crossfire, described in the conference program as "the culture war." While something like that war is going on, I am going to stress not a binary, bifocal, polarized, two-party conflict — as in "we" versus "they," "same" versus "different," "self" versus "other" — but, instead, many parties. Often these combine Christian and non-Christian elements, in constantly shifting, fluid, kinetic forms. One might say they represent "multicrossfires."

When people are told that they are caught in crossfire and that figurative shots are coming from many directions, it is possible but not profitable for them to ignore the action. There is considerable peril in ignoring and in ignorance. This conference represents an attempt to rise above inattention. Or they could be utopians who dream that through pacifist strategies those who are doing the firing can be outlasted. Who am I to deny the pacifist dream? Empirically, however, such a strategy has not been working. Or, third, people may engage in tactics of ducking the crossfire, finding places to hide. But the spray of verbal and organizational artillery is so intense that it is not likely that as many can hide as would like to. Again, a conference like this seeks alternatives to the great Christian strategy of ducking and hiding.

What is new in the current talk about "multicultures," and why are these present and firing upon each other and being reckoned with now? Any number of observers with historic senses remind us that multicultures are precisely what America *used* to have. Years ago blacks were isolated in slave cultures, Native Americans had no voice beyond the reservations and little there. Jews in the ghetto talked a Yiddish incomprehensible to other recent immigrants from Europe, who themselves formed "thick" enclaves, where different languages, religions, menus, wardrobes, and patterns of custom and ethos prevailed.

Today, for all the validity and variety of the survivals of these, counterforces have risen to limit the potency of these many cultures. Mass media, mass higher education, the mall, commodification, mobility, advertising, and the market have all worked to make more and more of these subcultures to appear like unto each other. Louis Menand has observed that the difference today is that in their samenesses these tend to be made up of people who wear their ethnic and sexual and religious preferences on their sleeve, making these a public issue. If you did *not* wear them there, you would really be different! Otherwise, everything blends. A magazine cover story by Benjamin Barber several years ago bannered a simple alternative for the world's future: "Jihad vs. McWorld." The multicultures try to withstand McWorldism, even as they often contribute to it. Yet here the multicultures are, firing at each other.

Again, why and why now? I like to look at the multicultures as being products of response to four needs in the late modern world:

identity: the need to answer, "who am I?" Modernity has been erosive of individual and group identities, so one stresses apparent differences in order to answer the identity question.

loyalty: the need to spell out, "to whom do I belong?" Whom shall I trust? The human race? The nation? These seem to be too protean, so I relate to my subculture as self-defined; it must provide the locus of loyalty.

values: the need to answer, "by what shall I live?" What do I pass on to my children? What would I like to see prevail in respect to the true, the beautiful, and the good? The larger society and culture are corrosive and confusing; my subculture provides the *couche* of values.

power: the need to answer, "how can I protect myself?" or "how can I make my way over against others?" How do I throw off the oppressor and how can I be free?

I consider these to be legitimate and understandable needs and queries and responses. There are good reasons why multicultures have become assertive and are firing at each other and at real or presumed oppressors, dominators, or other representatives of subcultures that are firing at them.

For all their obvious and presumed and claimed differences, however, the multicultures come on to those who are described as the oppressors — and these could be deans or public administrators, planners of textbooks and curricula or public events, legislators and judges, or stagers of parades — in some predictably discernible ways. They come presenting:

trauma literature or other such media expression, which is almost universal multiculturally. Usually it is true: the ancestors of and many contemporaries in the subcultures have been products of traumatizing events. The Holocaust for Jews, reservations for Indians, World War II "concentration camps" in the West for Japanese Americans, slavery for African Americans, exploitation in slums and sodhouses for Euro-American ethnic groups, exploitation of farm workers for Hispanics, and abuse of many women and children are among these narratives. Not to tell the story is to dishonor the sufferers.

victim status which is the result of trauma, and must be reckoned with, altered, exorcised, or dealt with in therapy and with measures of justice.

the name of the oppressor: naming the oppressor is always an act that is a part of multicultural expression. One finds identity, contexts for loyalty, centers of values, and political power by focusing on a dominator, an exploiter, usually in the form of another of the subcultures, or "*the* culture," however it is described.

cultural artifacts: literature, arts, protest movements, curricular and study programs are part of the demand. Interpretive communities protect these.

It is hard to look at the varieties of multicultural expression in America without seeing their enriching potential, the possibility of their being able to enhance the lives of those in other subcultures. However, in these days of crossfiring, they often come on not as enriching but as exclusive and exclusivist agencies and entities, which do not cross-invite but which crossfire.

This is not the place to detail all the multicultures. They can be made up of:

racial and ethnic groups, as in the pentagon of hyphenated peoples, Euro-, Afro-, Native, Asian, and Hispanic Americans in their own myriad varieties, and riven though they are with internal conflict;

or *sexual and gendered* differentiations, such as male, female, gay, lesbian, or bi;

or, of course, *religious* groupings, not only on denominational lines but ethnonationalist or ideological ones, as in "radical religious right";

or other *ideological* differentiations, as in animal rights, or environmental groups, left or right philosophies and activisms;

or *class* distinctions, often overlooked but most potent in multicultural contexts;

or even products of preference in *taste* or aesthetic contexts.

It is significant that Christian people are in every one of these subcultures that make up multicultures. That is why I am never able to see the "culture wars" on binary, bifocal, bivocal, polarized, God versus Satan, Christ versus Antichrist, we versus they terms. God and Christ and we may well be active, but discerning where and how this is so is part of the problem, not the solution, in human talk about multicultural crossfirings.

II. Possible Addresses to the Situation

Assuming that it is more creative to address the situation than to ignore crossfires, or to seek to outlast or duck and hide from them, we move now to discuss some ways of responding. The first step in response is to reflect on where one would go if one could go, toward what one would aim if there is to be positive reaction to crossfiring. I will outline several steps and directions.

1. *The call of the humanities,* which does not rule out the call of and to the social sciences, the sciences, and other liberal arts disciplines: I begin here because of the church-college base of our present inquiry, because of my own vocation, and because the humanities represent an area of potential destructiveness or creativity on the multicultural scene. "Christianity" and "culture" move through history with texts, artifacts, floor plans and dance charts and monuments, traces of human endeavor. Hence, the humanities.

However academics address these texts and residues with their various critical devices, their constructions and deconstructions, to the public the humanities represent endeavors to help us imagine what it might have been to have lived in the past, or to imagine what it might be to be someone else or somewhere else in the present. The humanities both represent the self and the other, the same and the different, my subculture and other subcultures. No wonder they are battlegrounds in culture wars, however described, also within Christianity and between Christians divided on racial, ethnic, gendered, religious-denominational, ideological, class, and aesthetic grounds.

Christians are concerned with the humanities, in elite and populist expressions alike, even though they cannot do "the whole Christian job." Attention to them does not save souls, make sad hearts glad, or answer the deepest questions of one facing death. But they are perceived by generous and grateful Christians as expressions of creative life lived under God. They allow for representation of the richness, "thickness," particularity of peoples and cultures. Through them one promotes either *enrichment* or *exclusivism,* and how one thinks of these humanistically and theologically will determine what kind of energies to devote to crossfiring, working for concord, or whatever. I promote a criss-cross pattern of approach to the texts of would-be exclusivist groups, as a subversive act.

2. *The call of politics,* for attention to the *polis,* the human city, leads one into the zone where crossfiring is intense. Most of the subcultures in multiculturalism exist for political expression. In our culture, not to speak up or organize for one's self means to be ignored or to be in potentially exploited situations. Women know too, as do Hispanic American gays, and the like.

Again, political life is not where "the whole Christian job" is exhausted. As one book title put it, "everything is political but politics isn't everything." It does not save souls, make sad hearts glad, and the like. It is the result of marvelous human invention by people who realize that violence, be it individual or corporate, is the dirty secret of human existence, that politics is a means of minimizing violence through cooperation, consultation, organization, rhetoric, and other not-always-violent means.

In this context I want to endeavor to offer a discernment that helps move us from the biparty, polarized approach to crossfiring, by referring to an elegant construct in my title: "cross-multiculturalism." I argue that we would be better off if we rendered formal our understanding of an evident feature on the multicultural scene: that most people belong to *many* subcultures, and that recognition of this and employment of the understanding can be a positive response.

Let me begin this with a personalization of this "cross-multicultural" or "criss-crossing" effect, outlined in 1929 by pundit and public philosopher Walter Lippmann. He spoke of "he" and included "she" and "her" when describing the person inside what was then called "pluralism" but today would be further described as being in "multiculturalism." Realistically:

In the modern world [the medieval] synthesis has disintegrated and the activities of a man cannot be directed by a simple allegiance.

Each man finds himself the center of a complex of loyalties. He is loyal to his government, he is loyal to his state, he is loyal to his village, he is loyal to his neighborhood. He has his own family. He has his wife's family. His wife has her family. He has his church. His wife may have a different church. He may be an employer of thousands of men. He may be an employee. He must be loyal to his corporation, to his trade union, or his professional society. He is a buyer in many different markets. He is a seller in many different markets. He is a creditor and debtor. He owns shares in several industries. He belongs to a political party, to clubs, to a social set. The multiplicity of his interests makes it impossible for him to give his whole allegiance to any person or to any institution.

. . . These allegiances are partial. Because a man has so many loyalties each loyalty commands only a segment of himself. . . . The criss-crossing of loyalties is so great in an advanced community that no grouping is self-contained.[1]

Such a person in this culture is not a prospect for becoming a fanatic — a fanatic being someone who in isolation spends too much time in the *fanum,* the shrine or temple, the sacred focus of identity, loyalty, values, and power.

Lippmann spoke of "criss-crossing of loyalties," and I want to enlarge upon that. "Criss-cross," says the dictionary, means "arranged and placed in crossing lines, crossing, crossed, marked by crossings and intersections." The etymological dictionaries will say that "criss-cross" is "a phonetic reduction of Christ('s)-cross," with Christ pronounced as in "Christmas." For my negative illustration, let me draw on some sociologists and observations in the secular *polis*. It struck me, for instance, that in the 1920s and 1930s "everybody was religiously mad at everyone else, but no one got killed." We did not turn out to be Lebanon or Yugoslavia. Why? Social thinkers observed that in America, thanks to criss-crossing, it was hard to shoot at anyone with positive outcome. Shoot at a Jew? Some Jews were with organized labor and some with management; if a laborer shoots a Jew, he cuts into his own force, as would a manager. Shun a Catholic? Catholics were Democrat and sometimes Republican. Would a vote-gatherer want to shun a fellow Democrat or Republican?

1. Walter Lippmann, *A Preface to Morals* (New York: Macmillan, 1919), pp. 268ff.

Now for the theorists who explained the process. Georg Simmel:

Contradiction and conflict not only precede unity but are operative in it at every moment of its existence. . . . There probably exists no social unity in which convergent and divergent currents among its members are not inseparably interwoven.

Or Jose Ortega y Gasset on Cicero's *De Republica:*

Far from extolling peace or regarding public life as a matter of suave urbanity, Cicero held *dissensiones civiles* to be the very condition on which the welfare of the state is based and from which it derives. . . . Have we not . . . seen that discord may also give the impulse for further development and perfection of the state? On the other hand [and here the analogues to Christian ecumenism and John 17 are obvious] a society relies for its existence upon common consent in certain ultimate matters. Such unanimity Cicero called *concordia,* and he defines it as "the best bond of permanent union in any common-wealth."

But most applicable is American sociologist E. A. Ross, who

pointed to oppositions within societies between individuals, sexes, ages, races, nationalities, sections, classes, and political parties, plus "religious sects."

He spelled this out:

Several such oppositions may be in full swing at the same time, but the more numerous they are, the less menacing is any one. [In other words], every species of conflict interferes with every other species in society at the same time, save only when their lines of cleavage coincide, in which case they reinforce one another.

Ross's metaphor is applicable to ecumenism:

These various oppositions in society are like different wave series set up on opposite sides of a lake, which neutralize each other if the

[22]

crests of one meets the troughs of the other, but which reinforce each other if crest meets crest while trough meets trough.

Is not this a picture of emergent ecumenism across the "many communions"?

A society, therefore, which is riven by a dozen oppositions along lines running in every direction, may actually be in less danger of being torn with violence or falling to pieces than one split along just one line. For each new cleavage contributes to narrow the cross clefts, so that one might say that *society is sewn together* by its inner conflicts. [Ross added that the result was] not such a paradox after all if one remembers that every species of collective strife tends to knit together with a sense of fellowship the contenders on the other side.[2]

Consider for a moment the connection between Christianity, the Christian communities, and the political order, and think of the *polis* in the zone of the interactive "multi-" subcultures. Johannes Althusius spoke of civil society as a *communitas communitatum,* and we might here speak of the church as a *communio communiorum.* Years ago Gregory Baum began to propound a vision of the Catholic church as "a family of apostolic churches," a definition which opened the way "for a greater decentralization than she possesses at the moment, and offers a theological foundation for a greater diversity in life and piety within the unity of faith and obedience."[3] Such is not the only, complete, or final conception of Catholic structure and authority, but it has patristic warrant and is expressive of the reality which has many positive features. Althusius spoke of the many communities as *symbiotes* which lived off each other and gave life to each other. So it is with the many communions, the *symbiotes* in the church ecumenical, as well as in the civic order. I argue that there is criss-crossing involving Christians and non-Christians on both sides of the multicultural expressions, and

2. Simmel and Ortega are quoted in an important chapter in Lewis Coser, *The Functions of Social Conflict* (New York: Free Press, 1956), pp. 72, 74; see also Edward Alsworth Ross, *The Principles of Sociology* (New York: Century Co., 1920), pp. 164-65. The emphasis is in his original.

3. Baum, in an essay in William S. Morris, ed., *The Unity We Seek* (New York: Oxford, 1963), pp. 1ff.

therefore it is misguided and misguiding to see them all on one side of a "culture war."

3. *The call to legitimate the order (or disorders) of the profane* in the multicultures and in and around the world of Christians. In conventional pictures of the culture wars, the Christians are defenders of and reliant on the sacred, and everyone and everything else is profane. I am speaking now in the etymological sense of the profane: *pro + fanum,* which means "outside" or "beyond" the temple. In much talk of Christianity and culture there is an impulse to see, in H. Richard Niebuhr's classic terms in *Christ and Culture* (New York: Harper and Row, 1951), that a positive outcome of culture wars would have Christianity triumphant. Christ would have "transformed" culture or we would be allowed to see "Christ of culture," a consummation of culture that would make it congruent with all that Christ wants and is. No: there are legitimate theological, philosophical, and strategic grounds to demarcate, legitimate, and with which to make positive use of this "outside the temple" cultural expression.

This thought was reinforced for me recently as I read Ernest Gellner's new book, *Conditions of Liberty: Civil Society and Its Rivals.* He was speaking of the "evil empire" side of the global culture wars as Christians saw it before 1989, Soviet Communism, which posed itself against Christianity in particular and religion in general. In Gellner's deft handling, Communism made the mistake of not allowing for the profane:

> The great weakness of Marxism may be not so much its formal elimination of the *transcendent* from religion, but its over-sacralization of the *immanent.* . . . The commonality of men require a spiritually stratified world, in which there is not only the sacred but also the profane. Everything may be sacred. But some things must be much more sacred than others. They cannot stand perpetual intoxication with the sacred (even if they like it intermittently), and they need to relax in profanity. It is perhaps this lack of profanity which in the end undid Marxism, which made its hold over the human heart so feeble. It has been said that society cannot make do without the sacred; perhaps it needs the profane at least as much. . . . So perhaps the world's first secular religion failed not because it deprived man of the transcendent, but because it deprived him of the profane. . . . By sacralizing the world, and above all the most mundane aspects of

the world, it deprived men of that necessary contrast between the elevated and the earthy, and of the possibility of an escape into the earthy when the elevated is temporarily in suspended animation. The world cannot bear the burden of so much sacredness.[4]

In a context appropriate for our present concerns, Gellner related this notion of the profane in a positive way to Christianity, Protestantism, and Calvinism:

Calvinism could have the effects with which Weber credited it by partially sacralizing work in a profane world governed by political compromise. It could not have done so in a politically *un*compromising world from which profanity had been banned, and in which there was no bolthole for routinized enthusiasts.[5]

In all this reference to Lippmann and Ross on politics and Gellner on the profane, I have left a large problem for those who are Christian within the multicultures. If there is to be criss-crossing of loyalties, what happens to the supreme, distinctive, ultimate, and total loyalty claimed by Jesus in the Gospels and depicted as the norm in the Scriptures and catholic faith? Does it not cancel out all other kinds of effort to express identity, loyalty, values, and power? Militant Christian movements of right and left alike claim to do so and organize themselves thus for potent participation in culture wars. Eric Hoffer once said that for a movement you may not need a god but you need a devil. In "culture wars" such groups have the advantage of knowing and pointing to the devil — who may also be a Christian who has many kinds of loyalties. How are we to address this?

4. *The call to participate in a variety of modes of existence.* The Jesus of the Gospels so particularly did this. He is sometimes portrayed in the mode of the banquet-goer, apparently oblivious to the call of personal sacrifice. At other times he does nothing but bear the cross. He lives in a variety of modes. For shorthand purposes here I am going to present a highly condensed version of what I mean by modes, using a reference

4. Ernest Gellner, *Conditions of Liberty: Civil Society and Its Rivals* (New York: Allen Lane, Penguin Press, 1994), pp. 40-42.
5. Gellner, p. 49.

to the work of British philosopher Michael Oakeshott, who observed "modal" life so creatively. Robert Grant writes,

A mode is essentially a particular, consistent way of seeing or conceiving the world, or the world as so seen; the product, roughly speaking, of a settled direction of attention. History sees the world under the aspect of the past; Science under that of quantity and regularity; and Practice under that of desire and value. Under Practice . . . [Oakeshott] includes both Art and Religion. . . . Every idea must belong to a mode; in other words, nothing can be apprehended except under some category or other. . . . [Modes] are really languages, or rather what are nowadays called "discourses," i.e. more or less self-sufficient meaning-systems within a broader meaning-system. [Oakeshott uses the Victorian term "universes of discourse."][6]

While I have Gellner's book open, let me revisit it. Coincidentally, he introduces a cultural concept similar to the "modal" when he speaks of the "modular" human being as a late modern development as in

modular furniture, bits of which are agglutinative: . . . you can buy one bit which will function on its own, but when your needs, income or space available augment, you can buy another bit. It will fit in with the one acquired previously, and the whole thing will still have a coherence, aesthetically and technically. You can combine and re-combine the bits at will. . . . With the old kind, if you want coherence you have to buy it all at once, in one go, which means that you have to make a kind of irrevocable commitment, or at any rate a commitment which it will be rather costly to revoke.[7]

Civil society and, I argue, Christian participation in the multicultural crossfire require what Gellner calls "modular man." This modular person

is capable of combining into effective associations and institutions, *without* these being total, many-stranded, underwritten by ritual and

---

6. Robert Grant, *Thinkers of Our Time: Oakeshott* (London: Claridge, 1990), pp. 38-39.

7. Gellner, p. 97.

made stable through being linked to a whole inside set of relationships, all of these being tied in with each other and so immobilized.
He can combine into specific-purpose, *ad hoc,* limited associations,
without binding himself by some blood ritual.[8]

What these "modal" and "modular" concepts mean is this: for one
set of purposes one participates, in one mode, in multicultural appre-
ciation and expression of conflict, on a pattern not of bipolar "culture
war" terms, with criss-crossing loyalties, complex identities, values
made up to include various humanistic and political concerns, and in
various coalitions. Without this, I would argue, you could not have a
college, a collegium, a university, a cultural presence.

Yet, when another call comes, as in a call to oppose injustice, untruth,
patent evil, in the call for the Christian to discipleship, one is in another
mode and all the multicultural interests fade or have to be obscured.
Yet the same person, without loss of integrity or of the ability to find
coherence, reverts to other modes when these are called for. Then may
come the time for what Gellner calls participation in "blood ritual,"
though such a believer never forgets that she or he lives in a world
where "specific-purpose, *ad hoc,* limited associations" also provide opportunity to live out the terms of the call to be faithful.

8. Gellner, pp. 97, 99f.

MIROSLAV VOLF

Truth, Freedom, and Violence

A Toast to the Past

"TO THE PAST," says Winston Smith, the tragic hero of George Orwell's *Nineteen Eighty-Four,* as he raises his glass to toast his joining the struggle of the Brotherhood against the regime of Oceania. Not to the confusion of the Thought Police, not to the death of Big Brother, not even to humanity, but *to the past!* His presumed fellow conspirator, O'Brien, who turns out to be a high Party official and his future torturer, agrees gravely: "The past is more important." For "who controls the past, controls the future: who controls the present controls the past."

Sometime before the encounter with O'Brien, Winston had scribbled in his secret diary a longer version of the toast:

To the future or to the past, to a time when thought is free, when men are different from one another and do not live alone — to a time when *truth exists and what is done cannot be undone.*[1]

As for the present, Winston knew that the Party "could thrust its hand into the past and say of this or that event, *it never happened.*"[2] When the

---

1. George Orwell, *Nineteen Eighty-Four* (New York: Harcourt, Brace, 1949), pp. 177, 29.
2. Orwell, p. 35.

hand of the Party was done with its cleanup job, the past "had not merely been altered, it had actually been destroyed. For how could you establish even the most obvious fact when there existed no record outside your own memory."[3] The Party erased, the Party rewrote, the Party controlled — the present, the past, and the future. On the surface, the toast to the past was a toast to respect for what happened, to deference for what we call "facts." At a deeper level, a toast to the past was a toast against the arbitrariness of the powerful who mask their misdeeds by denying that they took place.

The question, What happened? tickles our curiosity, of course. What drives our will to know, however, is not simply a disinterested desire to unriddle "a mélange of clues and codes" about the past.[4] If we don't happen to be paid simply to be curious, we will not want to play the fascinating game of decoding scripts and piecing things together so much as to attend to the much more serious business of establishing who did what to whom and why. Think of the families of those who disappeared in the torture chambers of the Latin American right-wing regimes. They want to know who the perpetrators were and what they did with their many victims. And they want the record set straight. Think of the citizens of the former communist nations in Eastern Europe. They want to know who the informers were and what the faceless secret service agents wrote in their thick files. Are they just satisfying their curiosity? Much more is at stake. By wanting to know "what happened" they are wanting to insure that the insult of occultation is not added to the injury of oppression as well as seeking to restore and guard human dignity, protect the weak from the ruthless. The truth about what happened is here often a matter of life and death.

For the same reason that we want to know, we also want to *remember* what we have come to know. Elie Wiesel concluded his testimony at the Barbie trial in Lyon with the following words: "Though it takes place under the sign of justice, this trial must also honor memory."[5] Earlier in the same speech he explained why:

3. Orwell, p. 36.
4. Joice Appleby, Lynn Hunt, and Margaret Jacob, *Telling the Truth about History* (New York: Norton, 1994), p. 259.
5. Elie Wiesel, *From the Kingdom of Memory: Reminiscences* (New York: Summit Books, 1990), p. 189.

Justice without memory is an incomplete justice, false and unjust. To forget would be an absolute injustice in the same way that Auschwitz was the absolute crime. To forget would be the enemy's final triumph.[6]

Erase memory and you wash away the blood from the perpetrator's hands, you undo the done deed, make it disappear from history. Erase memories of the atrocities and you tempt future perpetrators with immunity. Inversely, remember the misdeeds and you erect a barrier against future misdeeds. As Wiesel puts it, "the memory of death will serve as a shield against death."[7] Forgetfulness is damnation; memory is redemption. "Salvation," he writes, somewhat overstating his case, "can be found only in memory."[8] We may insist that salvation requires more than memory. But how could we dispute that there can be no salvation without memory?

Wiesel's obsession with memory echoes the biblical commandment to remember. As he himself notes in the preface to his book *From the Kingdom of Memory,*

> Remember. . . . Remember that you were a slave in Egypt. Remember to sanctify the Sabbath. . . . Remember Amalek, who wanted to annihilate you. . . . No other Biblical Commandment is as persistent. Jews live and grow under the sign of memory.[9]

Christians, too, live under obligation to remember because they live under the shadow of the cross. When they celebrate the Lord's Supper they echo the words of Jesus Christ: "This is my body that is for you. Do this in *remembrance* of me. . . . This cup is the new covenant in my blood. Do this, as often as you drink it, in *remembrance* of me" (1 Cor. 11:23ff., italics added). The Lord's Supper is the ritual time in which we remember the broken body and the spilled blood of our Savior. As we partake of it, we remember that night in which the "Lord of glory" was betrayed, humiliated, subjected to a mock trial, and brutally murdered; we recall why Jesus Christ was crucified and what the con-

---

6. Wiesel, p. 187.
7. Wiesel, p. 239.
8. Wiesel, p. 201.
9. Wiesel, p. 9.

sequences were. There can be no Christian faith without *that* memory; *everything* in Christian faith depends on it.

As we remember Christ's suffering, we are reminded to remember the sufferings of his brothers and sisters for whom he died. In the memory of Christ suffering, the memory of all pain inflicted and suffered is sanctified. The Lord's Supper, that profound ritual that occupies the center of Christian faith and symbolizes the whole of salvation, is a toast to remembering. Every time we hold the cup of God's blessing, we ought to remember the pain caused by the devil's curse.

What we have come to know we must remember, and what we remember we must *tell.* "For as often as you eat this bread and drink the cup, you proclaim the Lord's death until he comes" (1 Cor. 11:26). Just as the memory of Christ's death for our sins must be proclaimed, so also the memory of human suffering, caused and experienced, must be made public. Rosa Luxembourg is reported to have said: "The most revolutionary deed is and always will remain to say out loud what is the case." Now, all sorts of things may be the case, such as, that the cat is lying on the mat. Saying these things out loud may be trite, even a bit foolish. But in such cases the truth does not matter very much. When a regime of "truth" is imposed, however, when cultural mores, public opinion, or decrees of a totalitarian state codify what may or may not be said, saying out loud what is the case may indeed be revolutionary. If you say some things that you know are the case too loudly, you may lose not only a friend or a job, but even your life.

In the Old Testament, suffering was the basic lot of prophets. They "saw" what the powers that be told them they should not have seen; they said in the public square what others dared only whisper in secret chambers. Listen to Isaiah reflecting on what he sees and what people want to hear:

> For they are a rebellious people,
>   faithless children,
> children who will not hear
>   the instruction of the LORD;
> who say to the seers, "Do not see";
>   and to the prophets, "Do not prophesy to us what is right;
> speak to us smooth things,
> prophesy illusions . . ." (Isa. 30:9f.)

Why does Israel want to hear "smooth things" and "illusions"? Because she has put her trust in "oppression and deceit" (v. 12). The two are inseparable: if you oppress you will seek to conceal your iniquity by deception; oppression needs deceit as a prop. In Marxian terms, exploitation seeks legitimation in ideology. Blow the cover of deception and oppression becomes naked, ashamed of itself. Because power does not like running around naked, saying out loud what is the case can be a dangerous act of subversion. In a climate of deceit that concealed oppression, the prophets dared to see and had the courage to speak. This seeing and this speaking were the original prophetic revolution, if you please. Every other revolution rests on this one.

In Orwell's *Nineteen Eighty-Four* Winston Smith raises his glass and says, "To the past"! I want to join him and say, "To the will to know 'what was the case'! To the power to remember it! To the courage to proclaim it out loud!"

A Counter Toast

After I have finished my toast, tasted a sip of good wine, and sat down, someone who refused to take a sip from her glass may stand up and take exception: "Ladies and gentlemen, I suggest that the toast Professor Volf proposed is mistaken in two important ways. My first objection concerns *memory*. 'Salvation lies in memory,' we were told. But is all memory saving? Elie Wiesel, to whom appeal was made, was aware of a potential problem. In the same book in which he praised memory he asked: 'Isn't there a danger that memory may perpetuate hatred?' Listen to his answer and judge for yourselves whether it makes sense: 'No, there is no such danger. Memory and hatred are incompatible, for hatred destroys memory. The reverse is true: memory may serve as a powerful remedy against hatred.'[10] I presume no one would dispute that hatred sometimes distorts, even destroys memory. Yet does it follow that memory and hatred are incompatible, as Wiesel claims? By no means. Even Wiesel is not quite persuaded. Though he posits incompatibility between memory and hatred, he can bring himself to say only that memory *may* serve as a remedy against hatred, not that it *will*. History

10. Wiesel, p. 201.

is brutal enough. There is no need to distort memory by fabricating injuries in order to find reasons to hate; real crimes suffice. What resources does memory have, I ask you, to dissuade me from hating those who I know inflicted suffering on me or my people? You could as well argue that memory teaches to hate, that you must strike a potential perpetrator today if you want to prevent suffering injustice tomorrow.

"You see, it is important not only *that* we remember, but *how* we remember — with love or with hate, seeking reconciliation or going after revenge. Salvation, ladies and gentlemen, does not lie simply in memory; it lies also in *what we do* with our memory. Memory itself must be redeemed before it can save us. If you extol the virtues of memory, do not fail to tell us what will sanctify it.

"My second objection to the toast Professor Volf has proposed is more complicated, but bear with me because I shall be brief. The objection can be stated something like this: In addition to being careful about *how* we remember, we also need to watch *what* we remember. The power of memory lies in its claim to be true, in its implicit assertion that what is remembered actually happened. You will tell me, no doubt, that false memory has immense power too. And you are right — provided people believe the false memory to be true. Strip down the pretense of truth and false memory becomes impotent. The problem of remembering the past takes us therefore to the problem of *knowing* the past.

"We were told that we must know who did what to whom and why, that we must remember it, and say it out loud. But how do we know what is worthy of being remembered? You will no doubt say: 'Remember what happened!' Fair enough. But do not pretend that you can figure out what happened as simply as adding two and two. Let me remind you, ladies and gentlemen, of the obvious: different people see and remember the same things differently. Why are there different memories of the same things? Let me answer by giving an example from the recent past of the country of Professor Volf's origin.

"On the surface, the dispute is about numbers — how many Serbs were killed in Croatian concentration camps during World War II. Numbers, of all things, should be easy to figure out, one would think. Yet they are not. Serbian historians speak of seven hundred thousand victims; Croatian historians speak of 'only' thirty thousand, and add that Serbs have murdered as many if not more Croatians during the war. Croatians would tell you that Serbian historians inflate the numbers because the status of victim provides moral legitimation for past dominance and present aggression; as one of their leaders, a priest, said, 'Our power is in our graves.' Serbs would respond that, like any perpetrator, Croatians are whitewashing their crimes. And Croatians would retort that, like any victor, Serbs write history the way it suits them. As each accusation meets with a counter-accusation it becomes clear that memories are selective, guided by past and present interests.

"You see, the dispute about the numbers is not simply about numbers. Flesh-and-blood people are not figures on a white sheet of paper; when you deal with them you never deal just with numbers. Let me take for a moment a different example from the same brutal period in European history. Many more people would be willing to say that the Nazis murdered x million Jews than to say that the Allies murdered x million Germans, even if there were no dispute over the numbers of people who died in the course of the war. It matters a great deal whether one killed others in self-defense or as an act of aggression. And here, as you will no doubt agree, the questions of interpretation rush in. Who started what and when and why? There are cases in which we can give rather clear answers to these questions, as with the killing of Jews and Nazis. But most cases are not so clear. Indulge me to put things somewhat philosophically and then I will conclude: a statement that this or that happened cannot be isolated from a reconstruction of history that makes sense of such a statement. Facts and events need larger narratives to be intelligible; and since larger narratives are disputed, facts and events are disputed too.[11]

"Ladies and gentlemen, here are my two objections in plain terms: First, we remember what we want to remember because we know what we choose to know. Second, we do with our memories what we want to do with them because they themselves do not tell us what ought to be done with them. If these two objections carry any weight, the toast to the will to know, to the obligation to remember, to the courage to say what was the case, though well meaning, is profoundly misguided. What toast would I propose in its place? I'll give you *two* toasts and

---

11. Lionel Gossman, *Between History and Literature* (Cambridge: Harvard University Press, 1990), pp. 290ff.

you can choose the one that suits you better, or take them both, if you wish." She lifted her glass and, scanning the table, asserted, "To the truth of each community! To the truth of each little name!"

"Nice speech," I thought. "Even the toast was not *all* bad, provided you understand it rightly. How would I respond if I had more time than just to give a courtesy reply to the effect that our friend's objections are important and to a great deal right, that she misunderstood what I said, and that I nevertheless stand behind my toast for reasons that the present social occasion does not allow me to elaborate?" All eyes were upon me, so I stood up, gave my courtesy reply with a smile, and added: "I want to invite you to a lecture in which I will explore the questions, To what extent can we know 'what was the case'? and, How should we go about finding that out in situations of conflict? You are all welcome. . . ."

The lecture I thought of delivering would consist of two parts. In the first part I would want to make two *de-constructive* moves: one to discard a typically modern construal of how truth relates to history and another to do the same with a post-structuralist construal of the same question. In the second part I would want to make three *constructive* moves: one to suggest a rough outline of an alternative, another to argue that the will to truth requires truthful life which is in turn inseparable from the will to embrace the other, and the third to show that just as there can be no truth without the will to embrace the other, so there can be no genuine embrace without the will to truth. For lack of space here I will, first, simply discard typically modern and post-structuralist accounts of the nature and importance of truth and go straight to my first constructive move; I will suggest an alternative to the discarded accounts. Second, I will analyze the relation between truth and power in the encounter between Jesus, Caiaphas, and Pilate. In conclusion I will draw two implications of this encounter for our own search for truth between persons and communities.

Double Vision

The aim of our modern predecessors was, as Lionel Gossman puts it, "to disengage knowledge from power struggles and to disarm the violence of confrontation by establishing a truth of fact that would dissipate the aggressiveness of the pronouncements brandished by the parties in conflict."[12] The aim of many of our postmodern contemporaries is "to expose the manifestations of power and the confrontation of competing forces behind the notions of law, meaning, and truth."[13] Against the modern approach it should be argued that the "truth of fact" cannot be established because, try as we might, we cannot discard our own standpoint and perspective. Against the postmodern approach one should object that exposing the "manifestations of power" behind the very notion of truth in fact enthrones violence. If neither "truth of fact" nor "truth of power" can save us from the reign of terror, what can?

In his book *The View from Nowhere* Thomas Nagel suggests that in order to know the world adequately we must "step outside of ourselves" and ask "what the world must be like from no point of view."[14] When we distance ourselves from ourselves, "each of us . . . in addition to being an ordinary person, is a particular objective self, the subject of a perspectiveless conception of reality."[15] Nagel is aware that we can never quite succeed in leaving the "ordinary person" behind: "However often we may try to step outside of ourselves, something will have to stay behind the lens, something in us will determine the resulting picture."[16] Indeed, he suggests that a *purely* perspectiveless view — a view *only* from nowhere — would not even be desirable. For my own life can never be for me "merely one of a myriad sentient flickers" in a world that my objective self observes from outside.[17] Nagel concludes: "One must arrange somehow to see the world from nowhere and from here, and to live accordingly."[18] This seeing "from nowhere" and "from here" he calls "double vision."

I suggest that we keep the double vision, but at least when it comes to knowing the social world, replace "the view from *nowhere*" with "the view from *there*." We should try to see the world "from *there*" and "from

12. Gossman, p. 323.

13. Gossman, p. 323.

14. Thomas Nagel, *The View from Nowhere* (New York: Oxford University Press, 1986), p. 62.

15. Nagel, pp. 63f.

16. Nagel, p. 68.

17. Nagel, p. 86.

18. Nagel, p. 86.

here." To view a different culture "from nowhere" would mean to neutralize both our perspective and their perspective. This cannot be done, as Nagel would agree. Moreover, even if it could be done it should not be done; we can never adequately understand human beings from a purely objective standpoint. Instead of seeing the two cultures and their common history from no perspective we should try to see them *from both* perspectives, both "from here" and "from there."

Ideally, of course, we should see things *from everywhere* (which is what Nagel may have at least partly in mind when he talks about "the perspectiveless subject that constructs a centerless conception of the world by casting *all perspectives into the content of that world*").[19] For what happens "here" and "there" are not isolated events, but are a part of a larger stream of social events. "From everywhere" is how God sees human beings, I would argue. God sees not simply from outside but also from within, not abstracting from peculiarities of individual histories, but concretely. God's truth about the world is eternal, but it is emphatically not "nonlocal," as Nagel suggests the truth of philosophy should be.[20] God's eternal truth is *pan-local,* to follow Nagel's idiom. This is why God's truth is not simply one among many perspectives, but *the truth* about each and all perspectives.

In a creaturely way we should try to emulate God's way of knowing. Not that we can crawl inside the mind of God and see things from God's pan-local perspective. But we can try to see the other concretely rather than abstractly, from within rather than simply from without. What human way of seeing corresponds to God's seeing "from everywhere"? Seeing both "from here" and "from there." Only such double vision will insure that we do not domesticate the otherness of others but allow them to stand on their own.[21]

Seeing "from here" comes naturally. That is how we normally see, from our own perspective, guided by our own values and interests that are shaped by the overlapping cultures and traditions we inhabit. But what does it take to see "from there," from the perspective of others? First, we

19. Nagel, p. 62, italics added.
20. Nagel, p. 10.
21. Charles Taylor, "Comparison, History, Truth," in *Myth and Philosophy,* ed. F. Reynolds and D. Tracy (New York: State University of New York Press, 1990), pp. 40ff.

step outside ourselves. We examine what we consider to be plain verities about others, willing to entertain the idea that these "verities" may be but so many ugly prejudices, bitter fruits of our imaginary fears or our sinister desires to dominate or exclude. We also observe our own images of ourselves, willing to detect layers of self-deceit that tell us exalted stories about ourselves and our history. To step outside means to distance ourselves for a moment from what is inside, ready for a surprise.

"For a moment" qualifies the distancing, because after we have taken a step outside ourselves we will have to return, as we will see shortly. It is important also to keep in mind that when we distance ourselves from ourselves, we cannot step completely outside ourselves, not even for a moment. Not that we would have no place to go so that if we stepped outside ourselves an abyss would swallow us. After all, there is the world of the other out there; there might also be the tenuous "liminal world" that is born in the prolonged encounter between us and the other.[22] It is not for lack of space to go that we cannot completely step outside ourselves. It is rather that every place we go *we must take ourselves with us.* We can step outside ourselves, so to speak, only with one foot; the other must remain inside.

Second, we *cross a social boundary and move into the world of the other* to inhabit it temporarily.[23] We open our ears to hear how others perceive themselves as well as how they perceive us. We use imagination to see why their perspective about themselves, about us, and about our common history can be so plausible to them whereas it is implausible, profoundly strange, or even offensive to us. To move inside means to seek to come as close to others as they are to themselves, to get into an "inner correspondence of spirit" with them, to put oneself in their skin, as Clifford Geertz puts it in relation to the work of the anthropologist.[24]

Third, we *take the other into our own world.* We compare and contrast the view "from there" and the view "from here." Not that we will necessarily

22. Mark Kline Taylor, "Religion, Cultural Plurality, and Liberating Praxis: In Conversation with the Work of Langdon Gilkey," *Journal of Religion* 72 (1991): 145-66.

23. Alasdair MacIntyre, "Are Philosophical Problems Insoluble? The Relevance of Systems and History," in *Philosophical Imagination and Cultural Memory: Appropriating Historical Traditions,* ed. P. Cook (Durham, N.C.: Duke University Press, 1993), p. 78.

24. Clifford Geertz, "From the Native's Point of View: On the Nature of Anthropological Understanding," in *Local Knowledge: Further Essays in Interpretative Anthropology* (New York: Basic Books, 1983), p. 58.

reject the view "from here" and embrace the view "from there"; nor even that we will find some compromise between the two. These are two possible outcomes of the comparison, but other outcomes are possible, too. We could decide that we have to reject the view "from there." The only thing we do as we take the other into our world is to let another perspective stand next to our perspective and try to determine whether one or the other is right, or whether both are partly right and partly wrong.

Fourth, we *repeat the process*. Before the movement away from the self to the other and back starts, we inevitably possess judgments about the rightness or wrongness of the view "from here" and the view "from there"; it would be both impossible and undesirable to suppress these judgments. But no judgment should be final, bringing the movement to a halt. We can never presume that we have freed ourselves completely from distortions about others and deceptions about ourselves, that we possess "the truth." Every understanding that we reach is from a limited perspective: it represents *a view "from here"* about how things look "from here" and "from there." The modest goal we *can* reach is to acquire "a common language, common human understanding, which would allow both us and them undistortively to be."[25] And we must hope that our common understanding will in some way approximate the way the all-knowing God, who views things from everywhere, sees both us and them.

What happens *before* we have acquired "a common language," however? Do we just keep going from step one to two to three and then back to one? A privileged few who are paid to reflect can have the luxury of letting the double movement toward the other and back to the self go on until the agreement is reached. Those caught in the midst of personal and social struggles cannot. They must act. As Langdon Gilkey observes,

> Praxis brings with it *forced* option, one that cannot be avoided. When praxis is called for, puzzled immobility before contradiction or indifferent acceptance of plurality of option must both cease — for to exist humanly we must wager, and must enact our wager.[26]

25. Charles Taylor, p. 42.
26. Langdon Gilkey, "Plurality and Its Theological Implications," in *The Myth of Christian Uniqueness: Toward a Pluralistic Theology of Religions,* ed. J. Hick and P. K. Knitter (Maryknoll, N.Y.: Orbis Books, 1987), p. 46.

As we must act before we have resolved a contradiction, so too we must act before we have come to a "common human understanding, which would allow both us and them undistortively to be." But before and after we act we can and must see ourselves and others with a "double vision" by keeping alive the movement from the individual or social self to the other and back.

What kinds of attitudes toward truth and what kinds of character traits do we need to keep alive the truth-seeking movement from the self to the other and back? I want to explore this issue by looking at the encounter between Jesus, Caiaphas, and Pilate.

Jesus before Pilate: Truth against Power

Some of the most profound New Testament comments about truth are found in John's Gospel, especially in the drama of Jesus' arrest, trial, and execution (chaps. 18–19). I will highlight the social aspects of the narrative, concentrating on the relation between power and truth. This is not the only possible, not even the only important, reading of the text. John's primary intent, at any rate, is to engender belief in Jesus Christ, who is the Truth (see John 20:30f.). The soteriological perspective on truth has, however, important socio-logical and epistemological implications. The narrative itself invites us to draw them out since it moves both on a theological and a social plane: in deciding on the truth of the allegations against Jesus and his place within his social world one decides for or against "the Truth."[27]

During the trial Jesus is caught in the field of social forces with religious, ethnic, and political bases, all interested in maintaining and bolstering their power. The main protagonists are the Jewish leaders and Pilate. The Jewish leaders, who brought Jesus to Pilate, are afraid

---

27. For my purposes it is not necessary to sift out "historical" from "nonhistorical" materials in the narrative. I am reading the text as a *story* about the nature and significance of the commitment to truthfulness. My argument for the importance of telling "what was the case" (in a carefully qualified sense) in no way implies either that we cannot keep telling narratives whose point is not to tell "what was historically the case," or that we cannot learn about the importance of telling "what was the case" from the narratives that do not intend to tell "what was historically the case."

of his popularity.[28] If he continues his ministry "everyone will believe in him," they reason, and "the Romans will come and take away from us both our holy place and our nation" (11:48).[29] To prevent their own deposition as protectors of a nation and its religion, they plot Jesus' death and, as rulers often do, couch the desire for power in concern for the well-being of the people (v. 50). The rhetoric of benevolence does not succeed in fully hiding their motivation, however: it is better for *them* ("for you," says the high priest, Caiaphas) "to have one man die for the people than to have the whole nation destroyed" (v. 50). Between a whole nation with its venerable religious tradition (including its wise leaders) and a single man, the choice is easy.

Pilate represents Roman power. Most commentators portray him as a fair but inexplicably impotent judge who tries unsuccessfully to release Jesus. As Raymond Brown puts it, Pilate is "the person-in-between who does not wish to make a decision and so vainly tries to reconcile the opposing forces."[30] David Rensberger has argued, on the other hand, that we should see him as a cunning representative of Roman power who ridicules Jewish "national hopes by means of Jesus."[31] Though I think Rensberger is right, we do not need to decide here between the two interpretations. In either case, Pilate's goal was to preserve his own power — his hold over a province, his right to decide over life and death (19:10) — and the power of the Caesar. If during the trial Pilate acted

28. In analyzing the relation between truth and power by using the encounter between Jesus, Jewish religious leaders, and Pilate, I by no means wish to perpetuate anti-Jewish attitudes and actions that have characterized so much the Christian church's history. Since Jesus was himself a Jew, "Jewish religious leaders" in my reading of the text do not stand for a general category of "the Jews." The story of the encounter between Jesus and Pilate invites us to emulate *Jesus the Jew* by renouncing violence in the name of the commitment to truth rather than scapegoating Jewish people under the pretense of "avenging" the death of a wrongly de-Judaized Jesus.

29. For this reading of the text (instead of: "the Romans will come and *destroy* both our holy place and our nation"), see George R. Beasley-Murray, *John,* vol. 36 of Word Biblical Commentary series, ed. David A. Hubbard et al. (Waco, Tex.: Word Books, 1987), p. 196.

30. Raymond E. Brown, *The Death of the Messiah: From Gethsemane to the Grave: A Commentary on the Passion Narrative in the Four Gospels,* vol. 1 (New York: Doubleday, 1994), p. 744.

31. David Rensberger, "The Politics of John: The Trial of Jesus in the Fourth Gospel," *Journal of Biblical Literature* 103, no. 3 (1984): 402.

as a cunning procurator, then what mattered to him was not whether Jesus in fact had aspirations to a Jewish throne, but whether *people believed* him to be the king; in the world of politics, perceived power is real power and ought to be held in check. If, on the other hand, Pilate was a weak go-between, what mattered to him was to maintain his tenuous grip on power; truth and justice had to be subordinated to that goal. "One man must be sacrificed for the sake of my power and the glory of Caesar," thought Pilate. "One man should not stand in the way of our rule for the good of our nation and the survival of our religion," argued Caiaphas.

Notice the nature of exchange between the religious leaders and Pilate. It is a discourse of power. They bring Jesus to Pilate and want him sentenced because they have already decided that he deserves death. They give no arguments; they issue *demands.* When Pilate hesitates on account of Jesus' innocence, they *shout,* "Crucify him! Crucify him!" (19:6). When Pilate makes an effort to release Jesus, they employ intimidation tactics: "If you release this man, you are no friend of the emperor" (19:12). They do not even bother to provide "reasons" for their desire to see Jesus dead. The exchange of reason and counterreason, appropriate for the court setting, has been replaced by the rhetoric of pressure. That is the picture painted if we see Pilate as a mere "person-in-between." If he was a cruel advocate of Caesar's rule, as Rensberger argued, then he wins by shrewd deceit: he manages to have a popular preacher and potential troublemaker hanged and the Jewish leaders held responsible for the act; he succeeds both in having the Jewish religious leaders express publicly their allegiance to Caesar as their only king (19:15) and in making Jesus' fate a showcase to any pretenders to the title of Jewish king (19:21). The religious leaders seek to twist Pilate's arm, but he makes them executioners of his own hidden purposes. In both cases — religious leaders' pressure or Pilate's cunning — communication is a tool of violence, not an instrument of reasonable exchange.

Trials are supposed to be about finding out what happened and meting out justice. In Jesus' trial, neither the accusers nor the judge cared for the truth. The accusers want condemnation; they are even insulted at the judge's request that they name the crime: "If this man were not a criminal, we would not have handed him over to you" (18:30). The judge scorns the very notion of truth: "What is truth?"

he asks, and, uninterested in any answer, he leaves the scene of dialogue with the accused to return to the arena in which the play of clashing forces determines the outcomes. For both the accusers and the judge, the truth is irrelevant because it works at cross-purposes to their hold on power. The only truth they will recognize is "the truth of power." It was the accused who raised the issue of truth by subtly reminding the judge of his highest obligation — find out the truth. And significantly enough, he, the innocent and powerless one, remained alone in his interest in truth.

In the exchange with Pilate, Jesus argues against "the truth of power" and for "the power of truth." "Are you the King of the Jews?" asks Pilate. He means, "Are you a bearer of a power that competes with the power of the religious leaders, with my own power, and with the power of Caesar?" Jesus does not refuse the title "king" but alters its content. His kingship is not "from here," not "from this world" (18:36). The point of these denials is not that Jesus' kingship is not a force defining social reality. After all, he "came into the world" (18:37) and his disciples are "in the world" (17:11), inserted in the play of social forces. As a "king," however, he does not stand in the same arena with other contenders to power, fighting the same battle for dominance. His is not an alternative power of the same kind as the powers of Caiaphas, Pilate, and Caesar. If it were, his followers would "be fighting" to keep him from "being handed over" to his accusers who, in turn, handed him to Pilate (18:36). His kingship does not rest on "fighting" and therefore does not issue in "handing over" people to other powers. The violence of eliminating other contenders for power or holding them in check by treating them as things is not a part of his rule. In a profound sense the kind of rule Jesus advocates cannot be fought for and taken hold of by violence. It is a rule that must be given, conferred (19:11), and that will continue as long as one does not try to seize it.

Renouncing the power of violence, Jesus advocated *the power of truth.* "For this I was born, and for this I came into the world, to testify to the truth" (18:37), he tells Pilate. To be a witness to truth does not mean to renounce all power. For truth itself is so much a power that witnessing to it can be described as *kingship.*[32] As the one who gives

32. Paul Anderson, "Was the Fourth Evangelist a Quaker?" *Quaker Religious Thought* 76 (1991): 27-43.

the testimony to the truth, Jesus *is* a king. Is he therefore a threat to Caesar? Not directly, because he is unwilling to engage Caesar with Caesar's weapons. As Rensberger points out, for Jesus, "both the continued expectation of a revolutionary Messiah and the accommodation of the emerging Pharisaic leadership to the kingship of Caesar" were unacceptable.[33] But precisely in refusing the sword, Jesus calls Caesar's power most radically into question. "Caesar is king" and "Jesus is king" are therefore two competing and ultimately incompatible claims.

The power of truth is a power different from the power of Caesar. In a profound sense, truth is *not* "a thing of this world," as Foucault would have it. Rather, *truth is a power from a different world.* The instrument of this power is not "violence," but "witness." What is the task of a witness? To tell what she has seen or heard; her obligation is to tell it the way it was, to point to the truth, not to produce the truth. Much like language as a system of signs in Foucault's account of the classical tradition, the witness "exists only to be transparent." Speaking of himself Jesus claims, we "testify to what we have seen" (3:11); he spoke "the truth" which he had "*heard* from God" (8:40, italics added). A witness, unseduced by the lure of power, strives not to bring anything of her own to her speech; not seeking her "own glory" (7:18), she strives to point precisely to what is *not* her own. There is no better summary of Jesus' mission as a witness than his statement, "My teaching is not mine but his who sent me" (7:16; cf. 12:49; 14:24).

To be a witness means to strive to do the self-effacing and noncreative work of — telling the truth. That does not mean that a witness will have to situate herself "nowhere" and in sublime disinterestedness make perspectiveless pronouncements about what everyone and anyone must have seen or heard. Instead, standing at one place or another, she will tell in her own words what she has seen or heard. But though a good witness cannot and need not abstract from her particular situatedness, she will seek to renounce the clandestine imperialism of her own self-enclosed self which refuses to make space for the other *as* other in its cognition. That a witness will rarely fully succeed and sometimes not even try, goes without saying. Hence we keep suspicion close at hand even when listening to those whom we take to be good witnesses. But neither our suspicion nor witnesses' frequent failure alters the obligation

33. Rensberger, p. 407.

and the ability of the witness to respect the otherness of the other —
by seeking to tell the truth.

To insert "something of one's own" in the act of witnessing is always
a covert act of violence, maybe small and insignificant, but nevertheless
a real one. Jesus renounces such violence, because to accept it would be
to give in to those who define social interaction as a game of naked
powers. He would rather die witnessing to the truth than live manipu-
lating others by making his own agenda pass as truth. He would rather
have the truth carry a victory while he himself suffers a defeat than
trample truth underfoot and emerge a "hero." Why? Because the whole
purpose of his existence is to witness to the truth. Indeed, truth defines
his very being. "I *am* . . . the truth," said Jesus, adding that he also *is*
"the life" (14:6, italics added). The defeat of truth is the defeat of life;
the victory of truth is the victory of life. A man dressed in a purple
robe with a crown of thorns on his head, a man stripped naked hanging
on the cross, represents the victory of truth and life, not their defeat.
Should we be surprised that John considers crucifixion an act of *glori-
fication* (13:31-32)!

"This is naive," somebody could protest. "You make the Johannine
Jesus advocate the kind of objectivity that is both philosophically and
socially implausible! Do we not always insert our own interests into
what we see and hear, let alone into the act of witnessing? Is it not true
that social struggle, of which we are inescapably part, unavoidably colors
our perspectives?" We do, and it is true. Still, the objection is misplaced.
I have already underlined that abstract "objectivity" is not essential for
witnessing. Notice, furthermore, that the Johannine Jesus underscores
that the witness, even when telling the truth, cannot count on persuading the hearers; no rules governing the exchange between the witness
and the hearers can be designed to guarantee adequate transmission of
"knowledge." This, I think, is implied when, after stating that he came
to witness to the truth, Jesus added cryptically: "Everyone who belongs
to the truth listens to my voice" (18:37).

What does the talk about "belonging to the truth," or literally "being
of the truth," mean? That the witness is *addressed* to a chosen few? That
the access to the truth is restricted to the elect? During his interrogation
before the high priest Jesus insists that he has "spoken openly to the
world" and that he said "nothing in secret" (18:20). How else could
the one speak whose very purpose for coming into the world was to

witness to the truth? He spoke in public places — in synagogues and in the temple — where *all* come together (18:20). His testimony was public, open to all. His truth claims were universally accessible, inviting assent (or rejection) of all. The truth to which he came to witness was not restricted to his own community. How else would he be able to declare both his accusers and the judge guilty of misreading and misjudging his actions? "The one who handed me over to you is guilty of a greater sin" (19:11), he says to Pilate, implying that Pilate too was guilty.

Yet even if all could hear, not all did agree. In fact, Jesus implies that all *could not have agreed.* Why? In addition to hearing the witness to the truth, acceptance of the truth requires that the hearer be "of the truth," Jesus said. In John 8 — a passage whose anti-Jewish reverberations we must carefully avoid — Jesus contrasts those who are "of the truth" and ultimately "of God" with those who are "from the devil" and "of the lie." In a marked contrast to himself, who is the truth and the life, the devil is "a murderer from the beginning" and therefore "a liar and the father of lies"; when he speaks lies "he speaks according to his own nature" (v. 44). Those who are "from the devil" want to do the desires of the devil. Hence they "do not understand" and "cannot accept" the truth. Conversely, to be able to accept the witness to truth one must "stand in truth" and truth must be "in" one (v. 44). The willingness to listen to truth depends on the way one lives: just as "all who do evil hate the light and do not come to the light," so also "those who do what is true come to the light" (3:20-21). Hence Jesus can say to his opponents that they do not believe him, not *although* he is telling them the truth, but *because* he is telling them the truth (see 8:45).

The ability to know the truth is not just a matter of what your mind does — whether it adjusts itself adequately to reality or thinks coherently — but is also a matter of what your character is. You must have an affinity with the truth by being "sanctified" in truth (17:17). In the terminology of Michel Foucault, because knowledge of truth is never "pure" — at least it is not pure when it comes to the kinds of knowing that are more significant than knowing the phone number of your grandfather — but always already immersed in the multiple relations of power that shape the self, the self must become truthful before it can know and accept the truth. Since the self cannot be taken into a power-free space in which its cognition could function undisturbed by power relations, the self must be reshaped within the power relations so as to be willing and capable of pursuing and accepting the truth.[34] In this sense, truthfulness of being is a precondition of adequate knowing.

What about those — indeed, all of *us* — who are not truthful? Have I split humanity into a handful of the truthful ones, with the remainder enslaved in untruthfulness? Are the untruthful ones destined forever to walk in darkness because they cannot find what their eyes cannot see? In a profound sense, in order to know the truth we must be led into "the truth" by the "Spirit of truth" (16:13). Should we then say that the comprehension of truth is "not a free act of existence" but is grounded in "the determination of existence by divine reality," as Rudolf Bultmann did?[35] The opposition between the two is false — at least it is false at the social level at which I am here reading John's Gospel. All of us are always nudged by the Spirit of truth, yet only some remain in the truth. Those who do remain, says John, will "know the truth" and "the truth will make [them] free" (8:32).

Better than most people, Nietzsche knew what was at stake with the question of truth. Contesting the Johannine correlation between truth and freedom, he, in *The Genealogy of Morals,* insisted that as long as human beings "still believe in truth," they are "a long way from being *free* spirits." The "real freedom" can be had only where "the notion of truth itself has been disposed of."[36] Hence in *Twilight of Idols and the Anti-Christ* Pilate is the sole New Testament figure who commands Nietzsche's respect. The "noble scorn" of this Roman governor "before whom an imprudent misuse of the word 'truth' was carried on," writes Nietzsche, "has enriched the New Testament with the only expression which possesses value — which is its criticism, its *annihilation* even: 'What is truth?' . . ."[37] Whether the scorn for truth represents annihi-

---

34. The point I am making is not that there are no right and wrong answers which can be confirmed or refuted by evidence, but that you need much more than "evidence" and "procedures" to confirm or refute claims that significantly impinge upon human behavior.

35. Rudolf Bultmann, "aletheia," in *Theological Dictionary of the New Testament,* ed. G. Kittel (Grand Rapids: Eerdmans, 1964), p. 246.

36. Friedrich Nietzsche, *The Genealogy of Morals,* trans. F. Grolffing (New York: Doubleday, 1956), p. 287.

37. Friedrich Nietzsche, *Twilight of Idols and the Anti-Christ,* trans. R. J. Hollingdale (London: Penguin Books, 1990), p. 174.

lation of Christianity or an unwitting suicide of Nietzsche's own thought, however, will be decided partly on what we do with another kind of scorn which is the flip side of the scorn for truth, the scorn for human life. Nietzsche knew that by not taking truth seriously Pilate was deciding not to take "a Jewish affair" seriously. And he shared Pilate's scorn for the "little Jew" from Galilee: "One Jew more or less — what does it matter?"[38] Unlike Pilate and Nietzsche, however, the followers of the crucified Messiah must have passion for the freedom of "every little Jew." Hence they will seek both to speak truth and to be truthful people.

Truth, Freedom, Violence

Yet the unsettling questions remain. In a postmodern — post-Nietzschean — context, probably the two most troubling aspects of what the Johannine Jesus says about the "truth" are the double claim that one can "know the truth" and that "the truth makes free." What audacity to insist that one knows *the* truth! What naiveté (or is it malice?) to maintain that *the* truth will make people free! No, *the* truth does not liberate, our postmodern sensibilities tell us; it enslaves. The one big Truth is but the one big Lie made to pass as truth in order to garb the evil holders of the oppressive Power with the vestments of the holy guardians of the liberating Truth. To make people free we must disperse the one big Truth into many little truths. Deeply suspicious of any claim to the knowledge of *the* truth, we are comfortable only with the play of multiple perspectives. What can we postmoderns learn from that premodern interface between "truth" and "power" as played out in the encounter between Jesus, Caiaphas, and Pilate?

In conclusion, let me draw two implications of this interface for the question of competing truth claims in the struggle for individual and communal recognition. The implications concern the stances we should take in the search for truth. I need to preface what I am about to say by making a protective disclaimer to guard against false inferences. The first thing we need to remember as we seek to learn anything from Jesus Christ is that *we are not Jesus Christ*. Applied to the question of

38. Nietzsche, *Twilight of Idols,* p. 174.

truth this means that, unlike Jesus Christ, we are *not* the truth and we are *not* self-effacing witnesses to the truth. This is why we believe in Jesus Christ — to help us see that we are not what we ought to be and to help us become what we ought to be. Our commitment to Jesus Christ, who is the truth, does not therefore translate into the claim that we possess the absolute truth. If we know the truth, we know it in our own human and corrupted way; as the apostle Paul puts it, we "know only in part," we see "in a mirror, dimly" (1 Cor. 13:12). There is an irremovable opaqueness to our knowledge of things divine. Equally, there is an irremovable opaqueness to our knowledge of things human.

The first implication of the encounter between Jesus, Caiaphas, and Pilate is a disturbing insight that in an important sense *the truth matters more than my own self.* Jesus Christ was crucified as the witness to the truth. Sandwiched between the powers of Caiaphas and Pilate, this "marginal Jew" refused to place his own self above the truth — and became the Messiah of the world.[39] Why this self-denying refusal in the face of powers that threatened to crush both him and his project? Because when we put ourselves above the truth we open the floodgates of violence whose torrents are most deadly to the weak. If the truth ceases to matter more than our individual or communal interests, violence will reign and those with stammering tongues and feeble hands will fall prey to those with smooth words and sharp swords.[40]

But what about those who in the name of the truth oppress the weak? This brings us to the second implication of the encounter between Jesus, Caiaphas, and Pilate, which must always complement the first: *the self of the other matters more than my truth.* Though I must be ready to deny myself for the sake of *the* truth, I may not sacrifice the other at the altar of *my* truth. Jesus, who claimed to be the Truth, refused to use violence to "persuade" those who did not recognize his truth. The kingdom of truth he came to proclaim was the kingdom of freedom and therefore cannot rest on pillars of violence. Commitment to nonviolence must accompany commitment to truth; otherwise the commitment to truth

39. For a discussion of the significance of the cross of Jesus Christ for cultures in conflict, see Miroslav Volf, *Exclusion and Embrace: A Theological Exploration of Identity, Otherness, and Reconciliation* (Nashville: Abingdon, 1996).

40. Stanley Hauerwas has argued that to loose the hold on truth is to "submit to the order of violence." See Stanley Hauerwas, "In Praise of *Centesimus Annus*," *Theology* 95 (November-December 1992): 416-32.

will generate violence. The truth is a shield against the violence of the strong against the weak, I argued earlier. If the shield is not to turn into a deadly weapon, it must be held in a hand that refuses to do violence, I want to add here.

Our postmodern sensibilities tell us that to engage in the quest for truth is covertly to sanction violence; for the sake of freedom we shy away from the pursuit of the truth. Yet this pursuit may be less of a culprit than we think. It could be that we feel compelled to abandon the talk about *the* truth *because we are afraid to renounce violence.* But if we do not relinquish violence, the many little truths that we like to enthrone in place of the one big Truth will lead to as many little wars — wars that are as deadly as any war waged in the name of the one big Truth. The lesson we should learn from the encounter between Jesus, Caiaphas, and Pilate is that authentic freedom is the fruit of a double commitment to truth and to nonviolence.

"The truth will make you free," said Jesus. Free for what? In the light of my larger argument in this chapter, I will put it this way: free to make journeys from the self to the other and back and to see our common history from the other's perspective as well as ours, rather than closing ourselves off and insisting on the absolute truth of our own perspective; free to live a truthful life and hence to be a self-effacing witness to truth rather than fabricate our own "truths" and impose them on others; free to embrace others in truth rather than engage in open or clandestine acts of deceitful violence against them. For the sake of *this* freedom I raise my glass and repeat the toast to the truth with some hope that my imaginary interlocutor from earlier in this chapter will be able to join me because her objections have been answered — to the will to know "what was the case," to the power to remember it, to the courage to proclaim it out loud.

JACOB NEUSNER

Christmas and Israel: How Secularism Turns Religion into Culture

🕮   🕮

THE RELIGION JUDAISM affords no recognition whatsoever to the secular categories of race and ethnicity, any more than the mystical body of Christ can take account of ethnic difference among Christians; Christ is represented in every color. True, people think otherwise, deeming Christmas secular and identifying Israel with the State of Israel, or the land of Israel. As a matter of long-established fact Christmas in Christianity forms a religious celebration; "Israel" in Judaism refers to a supernatural social entity, God's people. But the Supreme Court declared Christmas sufficiently secular to take its place in the public square, and a great part of the Jews in the world have for two hundred years treated Israel as not a supernatural but a wholly this-worldly, secular, and ethnic entity, first "the Jewish People," now "[the State of] Israel." And "state" means not moral condition but political entity. In both cases, what we find is that the secular enemies of the religions Christianity and Judaism have taken over from within. How are we to understand the processes by which secularism turns religion into culture?

The process penetrates into the deepest layers of category formation, challenging not doctrine but the structural foundations of the faith. Let me explain by pointing out that the great monotheist traditions insist upon the triviality of culture and ethnicity, forming transnational or transethnic transcendental communities. The Israel of the Judaism of the dual Torah (that is, the Judaism definitive for two thousand years) makes no distinction between "children of the promise and children of the flesh," as Paul does, but defines "all Israel, to receive a portion in the world to come," by appeal to conviction, for instance, that the Torah comes from God. All, then, who affirm what such definitions of the faith proclaim and who practice what those definitions set forth come within Israel. Within the Torah the gentile finds no recognition; the gentile is fully Israel. The recognition of the Jews as an ethnic group, as distinct from holy Israel of the Torah, awaited the secular age, when post-Judaic Jews wished to retain the culture without the faith. But the culture was contingent, notional, episodic, and occasional, not universal, not encompassing. There is no one Jewish culture, so far as cuisine, accent and language, sentiment and attitude, and politics are concerned; but there is one Torah, so far as the Torah is concerned. When a secular Jew became possible and remained within the categorical formation "Israel," then Judaism confronted that process of inner secularization that has nearly obliterated the possibilities of faith within the category "Israel," meaning God's people.

Let me now generalize on this matter. Postmodernism affirms cultural diversity. Judaism, Christianity, and Islam mean to overcome diversity in the name of a single, commanding God, who bears a single message for a humanity that is one in heaven's sight. In the theology of the Torah, "Israel" stands for a supernatural entity, defined by appeal to valid faith; "the church" overcomes difference; "Islam" finds place for both genders and all races in perfect equality within the divine imperatives. To state matters in more this-worldly terms, the categories of race and ethnicity, critical in postmodernist discourse, represent secular and profoundly antitheological notions. Judaism, Christianity, and Islam all find exceedingly difficult the recognition that the social and cultural categories of ethnicity and race have bearing upon the authentic imperatives of the sacred community, whether the Israel of Judaism, the mystical body of Christ, or the nation of Islam. So far as the Torah addresses undifferentiated humanity and forms thereof its supernatural Israel, so far as Christ speaks to Greek and Jew, and so far as Islam forms the imperative for all races and both genders, no monotheist religion can afford recognition, or accord legitimacy, to the socially constructed categories of race or ethnicity. Not only so, but when

Judaism, Christianity, or Islam concedes entry to those categories, it is at a cost of self-secularization, the self-transformation of a religious system into a contingent, cultural entity bearing principally this-worldly and social valence. When we take up the matter of ethnicity in the context of Judaism, we encounter the effects of self-secularization, as a religious community redefines itself and in the process treats the uncontingent and imperative as instrumental and merely useful, commandments becoming matters of custom and ceremony, divine imperatives turning into mere folk traditions.

Two distinct categories therefore come together, ethnicity (inclusive of race) and secularization, for, as I shall try to show, the ethnicization of a religious community comes about within the secularization of religion, its transformation into culture. To a conference on the theme "Christianity and Culture in the Crossfire," the condition of contemporary Judaism makes a singular contribution. It is, specifically, to underscore the profound challenge to Judaic, Muslim, and Christian convictions that secularism presents in a benign form, as I shall explain. The challenge takes shape, in the case of Judaism, in such a way as to offer to Christianity (and, I think, Islam in time to come) the chance to peer over into the future. For most, though not all, of the Judaisms ("Judaic religious systems") that take center stage today show what happens when religion is transmuted into culture, the holy community into a secular social entity, and the religious calling into an essentially secular loyalty to the group. The power to disenchant the religious life and transform into something merely instrumental what for the faithful represents God's purpose derives, in particular, from the decision for essentially secular reasons to strengthen and make use of religion to work out problems of a merely social character and venue, political or sociological or psychological ones, for example.

To make this point clear and unambiguous: do I mean to say that when Abraham Heschel marched with Martin Luther King Jr. in Montgomery, he engaged in a secular act? Quite to the contrary: he understood his commitment, along with that of hundreds of American rabbis and other Jews, as an act in sanctification of God's name. A case can be made for a Judaic position on matters of public policy — a Judaic, not merely a Jewish-ethnic, position. That case is presented, to give one instance, by Michael Lerner (on the left) in his writings in *Tikkun;* by Daniel Lappin (on the conservative side) in *Toward Tradition;*

by David Saperstein, writing in the *Washington Jewish Week* (January 26, 1995), when he maintains that "in Jewish thought and history, the public sector plays a key role in ensuring justice, fairness, and equity." Saperstein turns to the Rabbinic canon to find justification for his secular politics. With these efforts, right and left, I have no quarrel, since I do not know how to distinguish proof texts from pre-texts. But where the state of Jewish public opinion is offered as the position of "Judaism," without reference to the canonical and authoritative writings and doctrines of Judaism, there I find the subversion of religion — in this case, Judaism. When we are told, for example, that "Judaism is pro-choice," meaning abortion on demand, I contemplate the explicit and authoritative texts of the Torah that state the contrary and conclude that Judaism has been made to adopt some, perhaps many, Jews' opinion as the norm; and that opinion speaks not for God in the Torah but for quite ordinary people altogether indifferent to religion but claiming the moral authority of religion.

To understand what I identify as secularism with a friendly face, let me point to how the civil religion of America proposes to sort out the issues of the place of religion in the public square. That is to accept religion on the condition of its secularization. The policy finds its concrete expression in the Supreme Court's declaration that Christmas may be accepted in its secular dimensions, "Jingle Bells" but not "Silent Night," Santa Claus but not the Magi. A second example derives from the conception that in a nonsectarian formulation, an act of prayer appropriate to the deepest convictions concerning that most solemn and difficult religious gesture may take place, thus prayer from no one in particular to whom it may concern: a you without personality or specificity. Yet a third instance well known to Christians is the secularization and de-sectarianization of chaplaincies, in hospitals and in the military for example, so that ministers, priests, and rabbis are interchangeable, without regard to race, creed, or color.

Now raising the issue of the transformation of religion into culture and the religious community into a secular, ethnic group — the secularization of the other-worldly in the interests of this world — may legitimately appear to cross the bounds of the postmodernist debate, moving backward into a world passed by. Harvey Cox's *Secular City*, after all, found its audience three decades ago, and issues of the secularization of religion and the death of God no longer provoke vivid debate. And yet, upon reflection, some may recognize points of continuity between the "culturization" of religion on the one side, and the shifting of the debate over religion to mostly this-worldly terms and issues on the other. When, for example, truth becomes relative, revelation is reduced to historical facts (as in "the historical Jesus" debates), and knowledge is treated as an expression of consensus, beyond all objective testing, then the conditions of the uncompromising faith of the ages — truth about God comes from God, through God's own self-manifestation (in Christ incarnate, in the Torah, to the Prophet, to take the pertinent cases of Christianity, Judaism, and Islam) — no longer pertain.

And that is by reason of an assessment of truth claims that precludes the very foundations of the religious affirmation of truth breaking from eternity into time. Even when critical movements that undertake a critique of secular theories and methodologies appear to align themselves with religious positions, the appearance deceives, since, in the end, the criteria of plausibility (not truth) find their definition within the secular and this-worldly framework of those critical movements. Rejection of "authoritarianism" extends to God's authority (however mediated), the very notion of commandment and divine imperative falling victim to the rejection of the notion of authority altogether. In these and other ways, postmodernism has carried to an extreme limit the initial premises and points of insistence of the secularizing movement in culture and politics. The "culture war" against religion did not begin this morning; it began with the formation of culture not only apart from, but superior to, religion that encompassed, also, the epiphenomena of culture.

True, some argue, in practical terms of this country's everyday politics the secularization of politics requires precisely the compromises evident in the re-presentation of artifacts of faith as instruments of culture. If Christmas is to establish any presence at all, better Santa Claus than nothing; so too with civil chaplaincies, so too with public prayer. Now in these compromises worked out for the sake of social harmony, Christianity loses its soul, conceding Christmas to be secular, the priesthood and ministry to be a mere this-worldly profession and not a supernatural calling, and accepting prayer that does not take place through Jesus Christ (to speak within the Christian idiom). In the academy, moreover, a parallel culture war against the specificity and authenticity of distinctive religious traditions, resting on revelation and a claim to unique possession of the truth, goes forward on another front. It is the homogenization of religions into religion, not for purposes of analysis and generalization, but in order to dismiss as essentially irrelevant to learning the specific traits and convictions of living faiths. Religions are presented as a shared quest, all equal; they are portrayed as essentially saying the same thing; their distinct messages are homogenized and strained into a single spread, with a uniform flavor. Here too the concrete and particular truth of theology, whether theology of Judaism or of Protestant Christianity, is set aside in favor of an abstract and general affirmation of what are essentially this-worldly commonplaces.

While, therefore, I realize that these concerns of mine, which I shall translate into the contemporary situation of Judaism, derive more from the modern than from the postmodern intellectual circumstance, I consider that the postmodernist challenge to the autonomy of religious truth stands in an unbroken line that extends back to the sustained war against religion ("superstition") undertaken by the Enlightenment. But, as I shall try to explain, in the case of Judaism we see a striking example of the war against religion in the name of religion. I point toward an attack upon religion from within, rather than from without; an effort to treat religion as trivial and marginal, rather than to overthrow religion through a violent attack upon, e.g., its insufficiency in response to the feminist aspiration or its ambiguous record in matters of race. Indeed, even invoking the category — secularization — may strike some as an effort to reach back to the issues of a prior generation, when the advent of religion in the secular world came to be celebrated by important theological voices of the day.

But the secularization of religion from within falls well within the framework of thought that treats all truth as relative and notional and episodic, all learning as negotiable, and all morality as instrumental. In the name of cultural diversity religious communities are asked to give up the right to make judgments of their own; in the name of a particular brand of feminism, religious institutions are asked to abandon arrangements of an ancient and enduring order; and so far as culture can be everything and its opposite, religions do find themselves compelled to take up opposition and to say, we make judgments, resting on revelation and reason, in favor of one thing and against some other. It is, I maintain, when the secular attitudes that favor relativism, negotiability, and instrumentalism pervade the inner world of religion that religion finds itself under the most severe attack, when, for the wrong reason, people find themselves doing the right thing.

Now to the case of Judaism as we know it today. Let me begin with an acutely contemporary moment, the discovery of religion as the solution to a problem of sociology and politics. To understand the phenomenon at hand, which is the secularization of Judaism, a.k.a. the Torah, for this-worldly, essentially political purposes, let me explain that, as everyone knows, Jews remain Jewish even while not practicing Judaism, the religion. They may define a personal religion, speaking in the oxymoron "my Judaism," as though a religion could ever submit to utter personalization and individuation. They may affirm their "Jewishness," denying the religion, Judaism. They may define a relationship to the Jewish community in other than religious terms altogether, that is, through philanthropy or through political support for the State of Israel. In these ways, secular Jews present a confusing picture for Christians and Muslims, who understand the distinction between the ethnic or national and the religious, even while forming this-worldly communities that express the transcendent faith.

The difference is, in the West Jews believed in the promises of the Enlightenment, affirming an undifferentiated humanity, in which even Jews might find a legitimate place, a community of humanity shaped by reason. Apart from a handful of intellectuals, the Jews stood apart from the rest of Western humanity in this perfect faith of theirs in the possibility of a transnational and cosmopolitan culture; the rest of the European peoples and their diaspora took a different route. They affirmed blood and iron, defining nationality as not territorial but ethnic, assigning distinctive traits to this race or that ethnic group, denying in word and (alas) in deed the premises of the Enlightenment concerning not the unity but the uniformity of humanity. Western Jews, in France, Britain, and especially Germany, by contrast, formed the notion of a secular Jewishness, infused with the values of international culture (art, music, philosophy, for instance). The ticket of admission to European civilization, they supposed, would be purchased at the price not of religious affirmation (as Jews universally conceived before the nineteenth century) but of cultural assimilation. That Jews founded the Universities of Frankfurt and Hamburg and London conveys the policy and program of this newly framed secular Jewishness.

[57]

One more set of facts will permit us to return to our own time. That concerns the response to the conception of a secular entity, the Jews, as distinct from the supernatural entity, "Israel," that Christianity had long recognized, along with Islam, as a transcendent social reality. The Judaism of the dual Torah set forth an "Israel" that found its definition in matters of faith. "All Israel has a portion in the world to come, except those who deny that the Torah comes from God" forms a definition of Israel in wholly supernatural terms, for example. For the entire history of Western civilization until the nineteenth century, "Israel" stood for that entity that various Christianities knew as "the church," that is, not a this-worldly ethnic group but a supernatural society projected into time by a purposeful God. For Christians, "Israel" in Judaism can be understood only by comparison to "the mystical body of Christ." While Christians understood that the churches in the here and now represent in this-worldly terms that mystical body, they also saw their churches as God's stake on earth. And so did holy Israel — and so do important sectors of the Jewish people today.

But at the very moment that "the Jews" took on social form outside the framework of supernatural Israel, the twin conceptions of ethnicity and race were taking shape, so that a general theory stood ready to make sense of what "the Jews" were saying to themselves about themselves. That theory divided humanity by allegedly intrinsic or innate, genetically transmitted this-worldly categories. Nations replaced multicultural empires, and races, once defined, took on innate characteristics. Ethnic groups formed territorial claims, with catastrophic results for the ethnic mosaic that covered nearly the whole of Europe. New nationalities had to be invented to take account of the result, Great Britain holding together the Welsh, Scots, Irish, Manx, and many other groups within the English-dominated framework, to take the oldest but least striking instance. And in that mix, "holy Israel" gave way to the Jews, who were given a social identity that, outside of the faith, had formerly found slight validation in shared traits of culture. Anti-Semitism as a political doctrine, with its match in Zionism as a politicization of "Israel," ultimately yielding the State of Israel as the sole point to which "Israel" would make reference, come together in two points. First, they concurred that the Jews formed a people, one people (in the language of Herzl). Second, they agreed that a single Jewish grandparent suffices to classify a person as "Israel," as the Nuremberg Laws stated in 1935 and the State of Israel's Law of Return affirmed some fifteen years later. Both stood for the radical secularization of what had for the entire history of Western civilization stood for a supernatural category and a theological position.

These facts out of modern history bear upon the postmodernist circumstance, because they help us understand why, in the name of the Torah, a.k.a. Judaism, one must insist upon the utter exclusion of all considerations of race and ethnicity from the community of Judaism, and, I would expect, of Christianity as well. Religions such as ours, which affirm the unity of the genders and the peoples in Christ Jesus, or the perfect equality and orderly integration of the genders and persons of diverse origin within the Torah, in the end can accord to the accident of birth no governing standing or even autonomous value. True, a child born to a Jewish mother is on that account classified as "Israel." But that fact rests upon the theological conviction, deep within the written and oral parts of the Torah alike, that the seed of the patriarchs is holy. The unearned grace of the patriarchs forms the inheritance of their children, for Israel forms an extended family. But children of Abraham and Sarah form a supernatural community, not to be confused with a this-worldly family.

Not only so, but the same fact — transmission of the condition of holy Israel through birth — competes with the superficially contradictory one, that a convert to Judaism enjoys exactly the same status, within holy Israel, as the child born to a Jewish mother; and as a result, the theological sense of the first of the two facts — indelibility of "being Israel" from birth — has to be discovered in dialogue with the second. But Christianity, Judaism, and Islam present in the end the denial that ethnicity and race and even gender bear within themselves definitive or indicative traits, and that theological fact forms the foundation for the religious struggle against secular ethnicity, on the one side, and biological or genetic racism, on the other, that secular politics today fosters. And all three great traditions of monotheism find great difficulty in mediating between culture and race and territorial nationalism and the claims of the supernatural community of Israel, the body of Christ, and the nation of Islam.

It must follow that when the monotheist religions accord recognition to gender, race, and ethnicity as autonomous social categories, classifications bearing their own intrinsic traits over against the traits accorded to all members of the faith community equally, they prove complicit in their own secularization; they admit worldly categories within the sanctum of faith. The result for Judaism proves so striking that the faithful of the companion religions will learn an easy lesson. To understand the case, we have to move from theology to the sociology of the Jewish communities in Western Europe and its overseas diaspora in the South Pacific (Australia and New Zealand), South Africa, South America, the United States, and Canada. In all of these communities young Jews have grown up within a secular Jewish culture framed by remembering the Holocaust, on the one side, and looking for meaning in Jewish existence to the State of Israel, on the other. This is a Judaism I have called "the Judaism of Holocaust and Redemption," or, on gloomier mornings, the Judaism of blood and iron.

For three decades now the answer to the questions of why and how to be Jewish emerged from the two mythopoeic moments: be Jewish so you won't join "them," that is, the gentiles, who hate us and will never accept us and ultimately destroyed a third of us; and be Jewish because of the State of Israel. Now, as a matter of fact, both reasons neglected the condition — as distinct from the state — of Israel, bearing no message for the critical moments of human existence: death, for instance; or for the chronic issues of a life: how to live a good life, for example; or for the enduring questions confronting any social group: who are we on our own, not in relationship to others? That is to say, the Judaism of blood and iron addressed a public and corporate community but ignored the family, the home, and the everyday community of the here and now to which the Torah addresses its imperatives. The Judaism of Holocaust and Redemption was formed in the model of the nineteenth century's nationalisms, treating historical events as media of divine revelation, and the nation as the successor to the supernatural social entity, whether holy community (the historical communities of Israel always called themselves, in their local and corporate being, *kehillah kedoshah*) or church.

What secular Jews have learned after these three decades of a public Judaism quite neglectful of the private life is, alas, that the coming generations found no self-evident truth in the Judaism of blood and iron — at least none with bearing upon the home, family, and everyday community. Consequently, at the critical point of continuity — marriage and the formation of a family in Israel, the holy people — the new generations in Western Europe and its overseas diaspora have opted out. The imperatives of the Judaism of Holocaust and Redemption — build Holocaust museums, support the State of Israel — pertain without distinction to whom it may concern. One did not have to be Jewish to build or visit a Holocaust museum (though if one was not Jewish, one would not likely pay a second visit to such a place); and if support for the State of Israel marked the measure of the good Jew, then successive U.S. presidents, from Lyndon Johnson onward, and Congresses for nearly half a century must claim the status of saints within the faith.

So the secular Jews, organized in philanthropic and political bodies and labeling themselves "the organized Jewish community," have today taken the measure of the received tradition of Holocaust and Redemption and found it wanting. Discerning the indications of an unraveling community, they turn to — of all things — Judaism. That is to say, they have formed in the United States and in Britain organizations to utilize the religion Judaism for the purpose of sustaining the organized Jewish community and persuading the next generation to continue to be Jewish, hence the name "continuity," used in Britain, and its counterparts here as well. Now to me it is self-evident that when secular groups wish to exploit religion for secular purposes, they are in for some surprises. The reason is that in the end religion bears its own autonomy; it is uncontingent; it is an independent variable; it uses, but it cannot be used. I would claim that theology best accounts for this unpredictable character of religion — to state matters simply, God in the end surprises us. But remaining in a this-worldly framework, it suffices to observe that when Jewish organizations discover Judaism as the solution to all their problems, the Enlightenment has run its course, and the formation of a secular Jewish identity, alongside of and in competition with the identity of Israel, the holy community of the God of Sinai, has come to its last path. The final solution to the Jews' problem turns out to be that Torah that knows not "the Jews" but only "Israel," as in, "The one who keeps Israel slumbers not, nor sleeps," a reference not to the Israel Defense Force's radar, not at all.

This brings us back to matters of race and ethnicity within the community of Israel, the holy people. The alternative to the received definition of holy Israel was the Jewish people. But the end of the Jewish people need not lead inexorably to the rebirth of holy Israel as the Jews' governing social metaphor. True, I have argued that the secular reading of "Israel" as "the Jewish people" has lost plausibility. But the demise of secularism does not carry in its wake the renewal of religiosity. For understood theologically, holy Israel derives not from the sociology of synagogue life but from the theology of the Torah. So far as the Jews wish to make use of the Torah (Judaism) as the medium for maintaining the Jewish group, the Torah cannot help them accomplish their goals. The reason is that, for Judaism as for all other religions, religion is not a means to an end but an end in itself. It is not, in the language I used earlier, a dependent variable, a contributory factor. Religion is an independent variable, one that explains other things but is not explained by other things. What that means is simple: religion uses, but it does not use, the facts of this world.

If people do not find self-evidently valid the affirmations of faith, self-evidently compelling the requirements of faith, then faith cannot come to realization for those people. If we have learned anything through two hundred years of militant secularization of the Jews, it is that, when originally religious attitudes and actions are taken over for worldly purposes, they lose their power; commandments presented as customs and ceremonies no longer compel. Truths set forth as preferences, convictions transformed into merely secular facts (as in "Jewish history proves" in place of "the Torah says" and "God spoke to Moses saying, speak to the children of Israel and say unto them"), lose all power of persuasion. The power of religion defines its pathos, its strength yields its weakness. What compels when believed does not even influence when not believed. Kosher when applied to food means, this is how God wants us to eat, or what God wants us not to eat; kosher when used to indicate a style of cooking that appeals to an ethnic group does not compete on a menu that lists, also, French or Italian or Chinese or Mexican dishes, and that is why kosher-style sells only pickles.

It follows that if people appeal to Judaism as the foundation for "Jewish continuity," as the self-styled "organized Jewish community" in the form of united Jewish charities contends should be the ideology of the hour, none will respond to that appeal for very long. Such an appeal — our ideology for being Jewish is now to be Judaism, as it has been Holocaust and Israelism — asks that the religion Judaism, or, as I prefer, the Torah, accomplish not the transformation of the Jews into holy Israel but merely the transposition of the Jewish ethnic group from one mode of ethnicity to some other form of the same secular ethnicity. But the Torah — Judaism — defies the Jews' ethnicity. The Passover Seder without divine intervention celebrates not God's power to redeem but merely Israel's power to survive — and the meal becomes a secular banquet with a quaint ritual. And that is not religion. The Day of Atonement speaks of sin and atonement, humanity's contrition and God's mercy. Turned into an occasion for the gathering of the clans, the rite is ritualized and loses its power to transform and to enchant. Having sat in a Conservative synagogue in Tampa behind a couple that was engaged in caressing ordinarily appropriate in the bedroom but not in a place of worship, I know that the widespread synagogue observance of the New Year signifies togetherness, but not a shared quest for God on the occasion of remembrance.

The broadly based American Jewish conception, therefore, that if only we build programs of "continuity" we assure the future of the ethnic group, represents a profound misunderstanding of the nature of religion. And that is because, in my view, two hundred years of militant secularism have left a huge proportion of the Jews completely uncomprehending concerning religion, religiosity, and the character of what the world calls "Judaism" and what is called, in its native category, "the Torah." The upshot is, what people do not believe, they cannot utilize. And that which they do believe to be truth stands beyond all secular utility. The retreat of Jewish secularism, the failure of ideologies resting on a this-worldly explanation of who the Jews are and why they should be what they are — these palpable events of the day do not open the way to a renewal of Judaism and a rebirth of Judaic religiosity, on the one side, and active piety, on the other. The alternative to secularism is not religion, it is nihilism.

To conclude, let me spell out why so secular a view of religion as the one that asks religion to carry out an essentially this-worldly social task profoundly misunderstands religion. A religious group is formed and sustained by people whom God has marked, to whom God has been made manifest; a religion records what that group knows about God. Religions represent what happens when people believe that, in what happens, God speaks to them, meets them, and sets forth what God wants them to do together. Those are, to be sure, convictions that can be manipulated for secular purposes, but they are not affirmations that

[63]

can be fabricated for the occasion. All religious people know that fact to be self-evident; and no secular people understand that fact at all. Forming and sustaining a religious community in response to the encounter with God is to be compared to dancing out music.

The matter is to be compared to the relationship of the dance to music. Martha Graham once said to me, "the dance is the physicalization of music." What she explained was, when she heard music, it would be in movement and gesture that she embodied what she heard. When in Chicago she saw for the first time the painting *The Girl with the Scarlet Sash,* she wanted immediately to dance the painting. And she knew just what she would do. Her limbs told her. Now, in the context of the religion Judaism, which identifies God's revelation with words written down in a book, and in the context of the kindred religions that identify book writing as a principal medium for conveying knowledge of God, Islam and Christianity, a book is the writing down of religion, that is to say, the encounter with God in time and in the present moment. Holy books, in the view of those who made, valued, and later preserved them as authoritative and true, record and preserve what it means to know God — as much as the dance records and preserves what it means to embody music. The metaphor then compares "know" to "embody." Encounter with God is not philosophical, that is, the mere factual knowledge that God exists, any more than the melody is the (mere) dance. Encounter with God is religious; that is, meeting with the living and very particular God who creates, commands, is concerned with Israel. But the knowledge of the encounter, recorded in words and in writing, makes possible our encounter afresh (so Judaism maintains concerning the Torah), just as the dance of the music makes possible the fresh re-presentation in physical ways of the melody.

True, the sages did not confuse map with territory, encounter through learning with the actuality of encounter itself, any more than Martha Graham conceived that the physicalization of music took the place of the music. The ballet would always begin with the notes of the orchestra (or the silent beat before the sound began), and the study of the Torah would always commence with the prior knowledge of God present in the Torah. The Torah is not God, the ballet is not the music. The encounter with God for religion, the music itself for the dance — these remain always other, but no longer wholly other and inaccessible, and that is what Torah-learning promises for Judaism's knowledge of and encounter with God made manifest in the Torah, as much as it is what the ballet promises for the realization of music. These are, then, remarkable and noteworthy writings, not to be reduced to trivial dimensions of whether or not a particular ethnic group, in the perspective of history barely a day old, survives another day or not. Ahad Ha'am stated the secular perspective, its profound incomprehension of what is at stake in the religion Judaism, when he said, "More than Israel kept the Sabbath, the Sabbath kept Israel." From his perspective, he explained why the Sabbath matters. But that is not the perspective of God, who said, "I am the Lord your God who brought you out of the land of Egypt, out of the house of bondage: Honor the Sabbath day to keep it holy." If people keep the Sabbath so that the Jews will survive, they will not have kept the Sabbath, whether or not the Jews survive. And so for Judaism. The retreat of secularism marks not the advance of religiosity, only the demise of the old gods. To the God who is made manifest in the Torah that event is simply not relevant. And Christmas in the end abides in the crèche, and not with Santa Claus.

PETER J. PARIS

Conflicting Spiritualities
in the Struggle
for Racial Justice

IN THIS ESSAY I will demonstrate how the struggle for racial justice on this continent represents two opposing worldviews the resolution of which remains unclear. Since spirituality pertains to the integrated network of fundamental values and perspectives by which people orient themselves to the world, conflicting spiritualities imply conflicting views of humanity and, hence, oppositional views about the locus of freedom.

Race, racism, and the struggle for racial justice have shaped the moral ethos of the United States from the beginning of its history to the present day. As a linguistic construct with no firm basis in modern science, the phenomenon of race has given rise to two contrary views of humanity, namely, racist and nonracist understandings. The principal function of the former view has always been the denial of humanity to the other on the basis of a logic that is incomprehensible to its victims. In the Western world in general and the American context in particular, racist views of humanity have been based on an eighteenth-century Aryan doctrine of racial superiority which claims that Caucasoid peoples are naturally superior to the darker peoples of the world and especially the peoples of sub-Saharan Africa. The seeds of this philosophy are at least five centuries old and can be seen most clearly in the historical facts[1] surrounding the mythlike account of American origins that has been immortalized in the story of Christopher Columbus, the so-called discoverer of America. The historical facts concerning that story reveal a graphic account of greed, selfishness, human oppression, and natural despoliation jointly authorized by the Spanish crown and the Roman Catholic Church.

Viewing his mission as profoundly theological and himself as the virtual fulfillment of biblical prophecy, Columbus went so far as to adopt the signature "Christoferens," which means "the Christ bearer." Further, his letters and papers are replete with reflections on the theological meaning of his mission.[2] In short, he viewed the territorial expansion of the Spanish empire and its increased acquisitions of gold and other riches as necessary means for financing a holy crusade to liberate the Holy Land from the Turks and to convert the world to Christ.[3] Thus, through Columbus, church and state were conjoined in a common mission of theological liberation through the imperial conquest of foreign peoples.

More important, neither Columbus nor his sponsors felt themselves under any moral obligation in their relationships with non-Christian peoples. Rather, they viewed the latter as subhuman, like livestock, to be done with as their discoverers saw fit. They were viewed as outside the moral realm and hence subject to arbitrary exploitation. It is a curious fact that Columbus thought of the native peoples he encountered as less than human while they viewed him and his people as possible gods, which, in turn, Columbus viewed as evidence of their childlike natures. While the native peoples sought to befriend the newcomers by willingly providing for their comfort, Columbus viewed their trusting natures as easy prey for exploitation and domination. Accordingly, he enslaved his newly discovered hosts, and in the wake of the decimation

---

1. I agree with the historian James Muldoon, who rightly argues that criticisms of the consequences of Columbus's voyages should not be undertaken in isolation from the historical facts. See his "The Columbus Quincentennial: Should Christians Celebrate It?" *America* 163, no. 12 (October 27, 1990): 300ff.

2. See *The Journal of Christopher Columbus,* trans. Cecil Jane with an appendix by R. A. Skelton (New York: Clarkson N. Potter, 1960).

3. See Pauline Moffitt Watts, "Prophecy and Discovery: On the Spiritual Origins of Christopher Columbus's 'Enterprise of the Indies,'" *American Historical Review* 90 (February to December 1985): 73ff.

of the indigenous population he imported African slaves as substitutes. Thus, he achieved the infamous distinction of becoming the father of American slavery, ensuring that America would not be the promised land for all who arrived on these shores.

Yet, it is clear that Christopher Columbus himself was not responsible for what we now call the "Columbus myth." In fact, he finally returned to his native land in disgrace and died ignominiously. Succeeding generations of European immigrants have perpetuated his memory as a pristine adventurer endowed with great faith and courage, propelled on his mission by the quest for novel spheres of conquest that would in turn yield abundant wealth and power for both the church and the crown.

The seemingly endless quest for wealth and power by the speculators of the new modern age characterized the spirit of Western imperialism in both its economic and political expressions. This spirit came to full visibility in the continental conquests of the Americas, Africa, and Asia by deliberate policies of genocide, enslavement, and colonialism.

Clearly, white racism was not innate to the peoples of Europe. Rather, its rise was stimulated by the motives of greed and profit made possible by the newly discovered technological powers of modernity and justified by the revolutionary changes in knowledge ushered in by what we now know as the Enlightenment.[4] Accordingly, countless millions of non-Western indigenous peoples were denied their humanity and pressed into various forms of bondage for the purpose of generating new material resources for the development and comfort of their Western conquerors.[5] Those who resisted this project were annihilated. Those who acquiesced in it facilitated their own commodification as slaves on the backs of whom the basic infrastructure of the modern West was built. No one has described this condition better than James Baldwin did in a 1970 open letter to Angela Davis:

4. A splendid argument in support of this thesis is presented by Cornel West in an essay entitled "A Genealogy of Modern Racism," in his *Prophesy Deliverance: An Afro-American Revolutionary Christianity* (Philadelphia: Westminster, 1982), pp. 47-68.

5. This notion of materiality as the basis of slavery, capitalism, and the spirit of Western religion was argued persuasively by Charles H. Long in a lecture entitled "New Space, New Time: Disjunction and Context for a New World Religion," delivered at the Moses Mesoamerican Archive and Research Project at the Center of Theological Inquiry, April 13, 1995.

We know that we, the Blacks, and not only we, the Blacks, have been, and are, the victims of a system whose only fuel is greed, whose only god is profit. We know that the fruits of this system have been ignorance, despair, and death, and we know that the system is doomed because the world can no longer afford it — if, indeed, it ever could have. And we know that, for the perpetuation of this system, we have all been mercilessly brutalized, and have been told nothing but lies, lies about ourselves and our kinsmen and our past, and about love, life, and death, so that both soul and body have been bound in hell.[6]

The most extravagant celebration of the so-called Columbus myth took place at the 1893 World's Columbian Exposition. In the context of structural racism, African and Native Americans were excluded from participation. Interestingly, Frederick Douglass attended as Haiti's official representative. Having been sent by Theodore Roosevelt as minister to Haiti and having so won the confidence of the Haitian people, the latter rewarded his friendship by inviting him to lead their delegation to the exposition. Thus, the only way an African American could attend that celebration was as part of a foreign delegation. The indomitable Ida B. Wells, however, raised sufficient monies from black churches, women's organizations, and other sources to publish a booklet entitled "The Reason Why the Colored American Is Not in the World's Columbian Exposition." With the assistance of Frederick Douglass she distributed ten thousand copies of the booklet to visitors as they entered the resplendent Haitian pavilion.[7]

Though the native peoples of the Americas, Africa, and Asia were not then or now moral innocents and though they also knew how to conquer, annihilate, and subordinate weaker peoples than themselves, none of them had ever constructed theories of natural superiority based on race. As a matter of fact, premodern societies seem not to have bestowed any normative value whatsoever on skin color. The philosophy of racism based on skin color is a modern construct that was bequeathed to the world by the romantic movements in England, Germany, and

6. James Baldwin, "An Open Letter to My Sister, Angela Y. Davis," in *Angela Y. Davis, If They Come in the Morning* (New York: Signet Classics, 1971), p. 23.

7. Alfreda M. Duster, *Crusade for Justice: The Autobiography of Ida B. Wells* (Chicago: University of Chicago Press, 1970), p. 117.

France during the seventeenth and eighteenth centuries, according to Martin Bernal. This racism pervaded the thought of Locke, Hume, and other English thinkers. Their influence — and that of the new European explorers of other continents — was important at the University of Göttingen, founded in 1734 by George II, elector of Hanover and king of England, which formed a cultural bridge between Britain and Germany. It is not surprising, therefore, that the first "academic" work on human racial classification — which naturally put whites, or to use his new term, "Caucasians," at the head of the hierarchy — was written in the 1770s by Johann Friedrich Blumenbach, a professor at Göttingen.[8]

Bernal also argues that while the ancient Greeks and others had strongly developed nationalist theories of superiority based on differing environmental conditions and although Aristotle has been appealed to by many to justify the idea of natural slavery, pseudoscientific definitions of race and their corresponding theories of racial hierarchies were developed by British, German, and French romanticists and not at all rooted in antiquity. According to Bernal, those philosophers also celebrated the importance of the American colonies and justified the extermination of the Native Americans and the enslavement of African peoples.[9] He also argues that the seventeenth- and eighteenth-century development of the Aryan doctrine of racial superiority provided justification for the Western conquest of the entire world which, concomitantly, denied and subjugated all Afroasiatic knowledge. This denial radically separates the modern age from the age of antiquity, which had long acknowledged the impact of Afroasiatic thinkers on the development of Western knowledge.

Interestingly, this nation's unsuccessful attempt in 1992 to launch a major quincentennial celebration of the Columbus myth symbolizes the immense cultural change that had occurred during the past century, coming to full public expression during the second half of the twentieth century. Worldwide changes were set in motion during the post–World War II period by the corresponding and interrelated freedom movements in India, Africa, and the United States. As the bearers of racial

---

8. Martin Bernal, *Black Athena: The Afroasiatic Roots of Classical Civilization*, vol. 1, *The Fabrication of Ancient Greece, 1785-1985* (New Brunswick, N.J.: Rutgers University Press, 1987), pp. 27-28.

9. Bernal, p. 28; see also pp. 201ff.

justice, these peoples ushered in a new era in human history by persuading the world to give formal legitimation to the claims of all peoples for political freedom.

Through centuries of chattel slavery, political colonialism, and economic deprivation, Africans on the continent and in the diaspora (along with Native Americans, Asians, and others) preserved their humanity. As survivors of the first Western holocaust, these people rightly deserve the type of celebration and reparation they have not yet received. Unfortunately, they alone must continue to exhibit the will and the courage to oppose the "myth of origin" by refusing to participate in the ritual practices of its devotees. And that happened to good effect in 1992 as Native Americans, African Americans, Hispanic Americans, Asian Americans, and others of goodwill raised their voices in public protest against an event that signified for them the terror of the American experience. In doing so they were demonstrating once again their desire to free the nation's myth of origin from its moral defilement of racism and its concomitant violence against human beings. To that effect, the National Council of Churches issued a resolution that called for a period of national repentance instead of the massive celebratory extravaganzas that were being organized at the time throughout the Americas.[10] All over Latin America tens of thousands protested peacefully against the proposed celebrations.

Clearly, the Columbus myth of origins could only be truly celebrated in a context like the 1893 World's Columbian Exposition, a context from which ethnic and racial minorities were excluded. That is to say, the Columbus myth could only be celebrated by its own mythmakers. It appears that the 1992 organizers were ignorant of the cultural changes that had occurred in the intervening century. Against the will of their opponents, ethnic and racial minorities had finally forced themselves into the full light of public visibility. Their voices of resistance pronounced the pending death of the myth in every arena wherein they could be heard and from which they were being excluded.

Thus I reject James Muldoon's conclusion, "To reject Columbus is in effect to reject the modern world."[11] To imply that the inheritance

10. National Council of Churches, "1492-1992 Resource," from NCC Prophetic Justice Unity, New York, 475 Riverside Drive, 1992.
11. Muldoon, pp. 300ff.

of modernity is intrinsically tied up with Columbus is culturally arrogant and logically flawed. Such arguments, however, abound among those inclined to see the whole of the modern world as derivative from the rule and conquest of Europeans. To paraphrase Professor Charles H. Long, the expansion of the Western world around the globe means that things of Western origin no longer belong to the West alone but rather now belong to all the peoples of the world who in their own way have placed their peculiar stamp of ownership on them and thus have remade them in their own image.[12]

The novelist Mario Vargas Llosa is right to say there is no way to know what America would be like in the 1990s if the dominant cultures were those of the Aztecs and the Incas.[13] But I strongly disagree with his main argument that the conquest of the Indians by the Spanish conquistadors was due to the former's inability to act against authority and express independent judgment and initiative, an argument that leads him to conclude that "They let themselves get killed" because religion lulled the people into a state of collective passivity. This is a gross oversimplification of the facts of the case, and it omits mention of the role that gunpowder and disease played in the decimation of the Indian peoples. The resistance of the native peoples was no match for the superior technology of their conquerors. In addition, although smallpox, diphtheria, whooping cough, measles, and other diseases claimed the lives of countless thousands of Europeans, millions of Native Americans perished as they encountered these Western diseases. The Indians had no immunity against such contagion, and their religion was hardly the blame for that tragic fact.[14]

Nevertheless, Llosa appears to be genuinely concerned about the possible integration of traditional Indian cultures with so-called Western modernity, even though he fears that the latter may well require the sacrifice of the former. Should that be the case, he says he would, regrettably, choose modernization over traditional Indian cultures because he believes the successful fight against hunger and misery favors

12. Long, "New Space, New Time."
13. Mario Vargas Llosa, "Questions of Conquest: What Columbus Wrought and What He Did Not," *Harper's* 281, no. 1687 (December 1990): 45.
14. See Geoffrey Cowley, "The Great Disease Migration," *Newsweek,* Special Columbus Issue (fall/winter 1991): 54-56.

the former over the latter.[15] Such an unhappy conclusion follows from his assumption that modernity is intrinsically tied to Western culture. On the contrary, I contend that Western culture is not a necessary condition for the exercise of modern science and technology. Rather, the latter two transcend all cultural limitations and consequently are potentially available to all cultures.

Clearly, this discussion raises a moral issue of immense proportion; namely, how America should understand the moral nature of its origins. Any true understanding of this question can neither limit itself to the history of Europeans on these shores nor legitimate the one-sided Eurocentric story of adventure, courage, discovery, conquest, and colonization. Rather, African and Native American peoples and others must be integrally involved with Euro-Americans in constructing the history of America in such a way that it can be owned by all American citizens rather than by those of European descent alone. In brief, the story of America can never be told as one story because its peoples have always been diverse. Nor can the stories of others simply be added to a so-called master narrative. As the humanity of each people is affirmed, worldviews must also change in order to accommodate the social practices that such affirmation implies.

Because the nation's foreparents were Native Americans, Euro-Americans, and African Americans, a condition of pluralism was present in the beginning, a condition pregnant with the potential for the creation of a broader and richer community. Because of their worldviews of racial exclusion, Europeans used their powerful weapons to annihilate most of the native peoples, confiscate their natural resources, and import millions from Africa as slaves. Such a wanton rape of humanity was the prelude to the destruction of nature, which also served the material greed of the conquerors. And, alas, the descendents of those conquerors do not yet live together in peace with the descendents of those whom their foreparents oppressed for so many centuries.

I contend that in the traditions of the conquered ones we can find the necessary ingredients for the construction of a new moral order. Clearly, a "new world order" can make no more sense in our time than it did in 1492 if it fails to be a new moral order rooted in a common spirituality concerned with the dignity and freedom of all peoples.

Admittedly, we do not know much about the genesis of myths. But

15. Llosa, p. 53.

we do know that they die through willful neglect. Consequently, every effort should continue to be made to prepare the nation for the death of the Columbus myth and its roots in the Aryan doctrine of racial superiority. In so doing, the nation would be taking the first giant step toward the restoration of the dignity of Native American peoples: dignity that has been incessantly trampled upon and nearly crushed to death for five centuries. Serious devotion of the nation to such a restoration project would be welcomed enthusiastically by all African and Native Americans because it would signal a constructive resolve to confront the racism that has inhered in the nation's history from its beginning up to the present day. Such a massive, national project would facilitate considerable in-depth analysis of Native American culture as well as comparative analyses of African American culture.

All of this would be contributory toward dismantling a racist myth of origin in favor of a more adequate national self-understanding. Such a process cannot be set in motion by extravagant celebrations of Christopher Columbus's ubiquitous plunder. Such public rituals perpetuate the infamous myth and denigrate both African and Native American peoples as a result. Hence, it is time to kill the myth. Such an act would be commensurate with the spirit of the United Nations's declaration that made 1993 the "Year of the Indigenous People." Such an act would be commensurate with the 1994 worldwide celebration of the death of the apartheid state of South Africa. Such an act would be commensurate with the death of Jim Crow in the United States three decades ago. Happily, the protests of Native Americans, Hispanic Americans, African Americans, and others of goodwill have done considerable damage to the Aryan myth of racial superiority, even though it is far from dead in our world. In fact, there are many signs that it is being successfully resuscitated in our midst.

In an essay entitled "Ethnic Studies: Global Meanings," Angela Davis reminds us that "While we have recognized the bonds linking us to Africa, Asia, the Caribbean, the Middle East, and Latin America as having been wrought by our respective racial and cultural heritages, we must be equally cognizant of the fact that these ties have been enormously strengthened by our common pursuit of dignity and freedom."[16] Davis goes on to note the peculiar correspondence between the

16. Angela Y. Davis, *Women Culture and Politics* (New York: Vintage Books, 1990), p. 186.

African and African American struggles for freedom. It is no mere coincidence that 1960, the year of the militant sit-ins throughout the South — which marked a turning point in the civil rights movement — was also called "Africa Year," because the colonial empires of Africa suffered decisive blows. Cameroon, Togo, Senegal, Mali, Madagascar, Congo-Kinshasa, Congo-Brazzaville, Somalia, Dahomey, Niger, Upper Volta, the Ivory Coast, Chad, the Central African Republic, Nigeria, Gabon, Mauritania — seventeen states in all proclaimed their independence in 1960.[17]

African and Native American worldviews have never been rooted in the hegemonic spirit of modernism but rather in holistic cosmologies that do not fully objectify any person or any thing in their respective communities.[18] Any such objectification occurrence invariably implies either excommunication or ritualistic death. Since all parts of the community must contribute to the well-being of the community, malignant parts must be eliminated for the good of the whole. For example, captives, including slaves, were incorporated into the communities of their captors. They could not conceive of the idea of having alienated elements in their respective communities. In contrast to the Western doctrine of Aryan superiority, these peoples sought to effect a common world between their captives and themselves. Since they viewed racism with moral repugnance, they, in turn, were viewed by their captives as potential threats to the social order because of their moral advocacy for freedom and dignity. African Americans sought to realize their goals through varying forms of moral suasion and public protest, practices that culminated in the rise of Dr. Martin Luther King Jr. and the civil rights movement he was called to lead. For more than a decade his nonviolent resistance movement rendered public service by giving persuasive moral fiber to the pressing issues of racial justice in the body politic. Their success in accomplishing what most considered impossible marked the end of an era in American history and the beginning of a new epoch filled with potentiality. That moral revolution in the legal framework of the nation produced the long-awaited birth of full citizenship in the Voting Rights Act of 1965, which enabled the descen-

17. Davis, p. 187.
18. For a comprehensive discussion of this thesis see the author's *The Spirituality of African Peoples: The Search for a Common Moral Discourse* (Minneapolis: Fortress, 1994).

dents of African slaves to became African Americans for the first time. These must now become the bearers of a more substantive political and economic agenda.

The struggle for racial justice both on the African continent and among African Americans has always been a moral struggle of the first order because its goal has been that of protecting and enhancing the quality of human life not for one group alone but for all concerned. In every generation of the nation's history, this ongoing struggle has been waged courageously and persistently by the victims of racial injustice and their moral sympathizers. Clearly, the moral quality of the nation's public life has been steadily enriched by that struggle.

Since racist and nonracist moralities are rooted in corresponding spiritualities, the struggle for racial justice must always be multidimensional in both scope and depth. Hence, legal and political improvements may or may not imply corresponding changes in either moral ethos or world perspective. Thus the problem of racism is likely to endure indefinitely into the future.

PART TWO

Feminism and the Possibility of Objectivity

NICHOLAS WOLTERSTORFF

Suffering, Power, and Privileged Cognitive Access: The Revenge of the Particular

FEMINIST EPISTEMOLOGY, Native American history, gay literary studies, liberation theology, Jewish hermeneutics — we are familiar with all of them, and with a good many other inquiries of the same sort. Until a couple of decades ago all would have been dismissed from the academy as inappropriate, if not disreputable. Today there's a thriving cottage industry in each. In this essay I want to reflect on why it is that in previous times particularist learning of these sorts would have been dismissed from the academy — and on the significance of the fact that it is no longer dismissed.

Let me unceremoniously reject the bland interpretation. There have always been controversies in academia — Aristotelians versus Platonists, Occamists versus Thomists, Newtonians versus Cartesians, Reidians versus Humeans, Hegelians versus Kantians, behaviorists versus cognitivists, on and on. The bland interpretation of the significance of feminist epistemology, Native American history, gay literary studies, liberation theology, and Jewish hermeneutics is that they are more of the same. But no practitioner of these latter approaches would think that the relation to the academy at large of his or her approach is that it is just one more example of an intra-academy controversy. All would see their approach as challenging the very basis of the traditional academy. I think they're right about that. The controversy of the Aristotelians with the Platonists was over the positions of the two parties on various philosophical issues. But feminist epistemology is not a *position* within the field of epistemology. It's not comparable to a coherentist theory of justified belief, nor to a representationalist theory of perception, nor to any other such *position* within the field. Better to think of it as a *perspective* on the field of epistemology — a way of thinking about the field, a way of approaching it, a slant on it. Further, the perspective in question is a way of looking at many other fields as well, not just epistemology; and it is identified not by naming someone who happens to have developed it but by specifying those for whom this comprehensive perspective on things is a significant part of their own narrative identity. To set out to develop a feminist perspective on epistemology is not to set out to articulate a certain *position* on one of the contested issues within epistemology but to set out to discover how the field as a whole looks when this aspect of one's narrative identity is allowed to function as perspective.

Far and away the most common interpretation nowadays of the rise of particularist perspectival learning is the following. Historically, white, Western, upper middle-class, heterosexual males have occupied a position of hegemony in the academy. A crucial element in the strategy they have employed for securing their hegemony has been presenting themselves as having thrown off all particularist perspectives so as to engage in scholarship simply as generic human beings. Theirs is a view on the world from nowhere in particular by The Human Being Itself. In fact, however, they have conducted their scholarship within the perspective characteristic of their identity — that of white, Western, upper middle-class, heterosexual males. Equity demands that their hegemonic grip on the academy be broken and that the academy be opened up to the representatives of any particularist perspective who have something interesting to say.

This, I say, is nowadays much the most common interpretation. And almost always the context for the interpretation is an eager embrace of metaphysical antirealism. There is no ready-made world; things exist and propositions are true only relative to a particular conceptual scheme. And the decision as to which scheme to adopt can in the last resort be made only by reference to which best serves one's interests. But we differ in our interests. Accordingly, the academy at bottom is a vast constellation of interests contesting for power.

I think we are all in debt to those who have espoused this interpretation of what transpires in the academy. They have had their eye on something real and important. Those who have traditionally undertaken to speak on behalf of the academy have presented the academy otherwise; but it is in fact a locus of struggles for power in the service of interests. The response of Christians in particular to this fact should be: "So what's new? Exactly what we would have expected!" The academy is like all other social institutions in that it participates in the fallenness of our human existence rather than being lifted above it.

But to say that those who espouse this interpretation have their eye on something real and important is by no means to say that the interpretation they have offered of what they have discerned is correct and worthy of acceptance. It should, in my judgment, be firmly rejected. Though not without insight, it is nonetheless glibly vulgar Marxism; and its antirealism I regard as untenable. It's true that in the academy's rejection of such particularist perspectives as feminism and liberationism, its own interests are at work. But to suppose that that is the whole of the matter — that it's all nothing more than self-interested power exercised with false consciousness — is appallingly imperceptive.

What has also been at work is the grip on the human imagination, from the classical Greeks on into the contemporary world, of what I shall call the "Grand Project." The academy, until very recently, has always rejected anything like feminist epistemology, Native American history, gay literary studies, liberation theology, and Jewish hermeneutics. "Anything like," I say. It has also rejected learning conducted from the particularist perspective of white, Western, heterosexual males belonging to the power structure of society. That is to say: though in practice it no doubt engaged in such learning, *officially* it rejected it. The Grand Project to which the academy has for millennia been committed — in profession if not always in practice — is incompatible with all particularist perspectival learning. Those who engage in particularist perspectival learning within the academy are right to see themselves as challenging the very basis of the traditional academy, rather than merely espousing a position on some of the issues under debate within the traditional academy. But what they are challenging is not just the hegemony and false consciousness of a certain party within the academy, but the visionary project which for millennia has inspired the academy. The false consciousness presupposes that ideal; if that project had no grip on our imagination, the attempt to justify what one was doing — be it made in false consciousness or not — by pleading that one was engaged in that project would fall on bewildered ears.

Begin by noticing that from Plato onwards, the standard imagery for what one does when entering the academy and engaging in *Wissenschaft* is that of *turning away* from the everyday. It would be possible to think of what transpires in the academy as the extension and intensification of what transpires in the everyday. In fact the dominant image has always been that of departure. One leaves the everyday behind so as to go into another land.

Take a line, says Plato in the sixth book of the *Republic,* and divide it into two (unequal) segments. Let one segment represent the perceptible; the other, the intelligible. Then divide each of these segments in turn. Of that initial segment which represents the perceptible, let one part represent the appearances of perceptible things; the other, the perceptible things themselves. And of that initial segment which represents the intelligible, let one part represent things knowable only by inference from things known, perhaps with the assistance of perceptible illustrations; let the other part represent things knowable immediately and without the assistance of illustrations. We can then pair off modes of intellectual activity with these different parts of the line and what they represent. There will be imagining *(eikasia)* and believing *(pistis)* corresponding to the two parts of the first segment, these together constituting opinion *(doxa);* and there will be thinking *(dianoia)* and knowing *(episteme)* corresponding to the two parts of the second segment.

Plato's instruction, *take a divided line and let its parts represent,* opens with language which is nonevaluative. He does not say, "let the *lower* part of the line represent. . . ." He says simply, "take a line divided into two unequal parts, one to represent. . . ." But anyone who has read this far in the *Republic* knows Plato's assessment of *doxa* and *episteme.* And by the time we are instructed to pair off mental states or actions with the parts of the line and what they symbolize, the evaluation has become fully explicit: "take, as corresponding to the four sections, these four states of mind: *intelligence* for the highest, *thinking* for the second, *belief* for the third, and for the last *imagining.* These you may arrange as the terms in a proportion, assigning to each a degree of clearness and certainty corresponding to the measure in which their objects possess truth and reality."[1]

Episteme is highest; *doxa,* in its two forms, is lowest. For *episteme* occurs when we are in touch with what is fully real: with the realm of the necessary, eternal, immutable. Plato postulated the presence in us human beings of a faculty which puts us in touch with necessity: the faculty of reason. In the *Timaeus* Plato argued that apprehension of the contingent can never be certain; only apprehension of the necessary can be that. *Episteme* is certain; *doxa,* uncertain. For Plato, the "moral" was clear: the ideal activity is the activity of *theoria,* contemplation of the realm of the eternal and necessary, retaining only so much of *doxa* as is unavoidable. And the academy is the institutional locus for that activity of *theoria.*

Whitehead once remarked that Western philosophy is little more than a series of footnotes to Plato. On no point is that more true than on the point in hand. Let me mention a few of the footnotes. By the time we get to the medieval Aristotelianism represented by Aquinas, the practices Plato recommended for the exercise of *theoria* had been crystallized into the project of *scientia.* In *scientia* we start from what is or has been evident — preferably self-evident — to some rational being or other, and we proceed to draw inferences, preferably by deduction. *Scientia* proper consists of the conclusions arrived at; it is the superstructure erected on the foundation of what is or was evident. As to *doxa,* however, Aquinas's conclusion was that Plato's response was too monolithic, too lacking in nuance. Very much of *doxa* we must leave behind when we enter the academy. But not all. We do not leave behind the texts which have been handed down to us. We discard a few as irredeemably heretical. But for the rest, we employ strategies of interpretation so as to extract from them the articulate wisdom that as a totality they contain. The result is still *doxa* — not *scientia.* But it is a higher form of *doxa* from that which we find in the everyday. It's true that *scientia* is nobler than the wisdom which emerges from the dialectical interpretation of the textual tradition. But to discard such wisdom would be an irreplaceable loss. To which must be added that there is

---

1. Plato, *Republic,* trans. F. M. Cornford (Oxford: Oxford University Press, 1945), p. 511.

no better preparation for engaging in *scientia* than just exactly such dialectics.

Descartes, to leap some four hundred years, sided more with Plato in this debate than with the medieval Aristotelians. He had no disagreement with the medievals on their ideal of *scientia;* in fact, he devoted his entire career to breathing new life into that ideal. But he disagreed firmly with them on their estimation of the worth of the textual tradition. Close all the books, said Descartes. No doubt there's some truth contained therein. But everybody agrees that the ideal of the academy is the project of *scientia.* And rather than dialectical interpretation of the textual tradition being the best preparation for the practice of *scientia,* it is very nearly the worst. The practice of *scientia* requires that one be clear, at the beginning, as to what is evident to one — what is certain for one. The reading of books, rather than clarifying one's mind on this matter, introduces all sorts of *praejudicia.* It makes us *think* things are certain for us when they are not. Practice instead the Therapy of Doubt.

John Locke, and his Royal Society cohorts in the seventeenth century, composed yet a different series of footnotes. Though the traditional concept of *scientia* was still to be found in Locke's conceptual arsenal, and though Locke was as convinced as were his predecessors of the nobility of the project, he no longer thought it came to much. Mathematics was a *scientia,* perhaps moral theory could eventually take the form of a *scientia;* but that was about it. Yet the image of departing from the everyday as one entered the academy was as present in Locke as in anyone. Obviously it wasn't *doxa* that one departed from; as Locke saw it, to depart from *doxa* would be to leave the academy almost entirely depopulated. So far, then, Locke was in agreement with the medieval Aristotelians. But most emphatically he did not think that the academy should supplement its meager exercise of *scientia* with the interpretation of texts. Locke followed Descartes in insisting on the closing of the books. In entering the academy one leaves behind the everyday ways of arriving at *doxa,* so as to employ a new and better way of arriving at *doxa* — the *best* way, the *optimal* practice. It goes like this: when the issue arises of whether or not to believe some proposition, one assembles a satisfactory body of evidence consisting of beliefs of which one is certain because the corresponding facts are evident to one; then one calculates the probability of the proposition on that evidence; and finally one believes or disbelieves with a firmness proportioned to that probability. The result will usually still be *doxa*. But it will be *doxa* firmly grounded, as the *doxa* of the everyday is not.

It would be easy to go on in this fashion, citing more such footnotes; but let me halt, since the point is now clear. From Plato on into the contemporary world, entering the academy is described as departing from the everyday so as to engage in something better. On what exactly constitutes that "better," there has been disagreement, as there has on what exactly one is leaving behind. But the image of *departure* is pervasive — departure from the everyday for something not just different but better.

Thus far I have emphasized the different ways in which other and better was understood. But we must not allow the differences to obscure a fundamental continuity. For my purposes on this occasion, the continuity is more important than the differences. From Plato onwards, what transpires in the academy is seen as better than the everyday because it is *more objective* and *better grounded*. We nowadays are mightily impressed with the expansion of knowledge which the academy affords us. I daresay that most people, if asked to reflect on why that is so, would say that it has something to do with the fact that the practices of the academy are more objective and better grounded than those in ordinary life.

Objectivity is a Janus-faced concept. On the one side, it denotes being genuinely in touch with the object, with what's objectively there, with what's out there. On the other side, it means being impartial, not reflecting one or another particular perspective on what's out there but approaching it simply as a perceptive human being. These two sides of the concept are connected; otherwise they wouldn't be two sides of one concept but two concepts. The connection is the assumption that to get genuinely in touch with the object, or to do so in a more reliable way, one must eliminate the particularity of one's perspective. The assumption is that particularity represents bias, prejudice, obstruction. And the better groundedness of what transpires in the academy is understood as connected with its greater objectivity. Removing one's biases and genuinely and reliably getting in touch with the object is what yields groundedness.

To understand this with any depth at all we'll have to dip our toes into a bit of epistemology. The dominant picture which comes to mind when reading contemporary epistemology in the analytic tradition, and its antecedents in modern philosophy, is that of a solitary person sitting in a chair passively receiving such sensory stimulation as comes his way, taking note of the beliefs which that stimulation forms in him, recalling certain events from his past, observing what is going on in his mind, and drawing inferences. It's the epistemology of a *reactor,* of someone who receives stimulation and then goes off on his own interior course of thought. It's the epistemology of a *solitary* reactor, for almost no attention is paid to other persons — to the role of testimony in our lives, for example. And it's the epistemology of an *immobile* solitary reactor. Paraplegic epistemology. The body enters the picture only so far as sensory stimulation requires a body. And even that requirement is treated as a contingency — witness the popularity of thought-experiments in which all that's left of the body is the brain.

Now compare. To be sure of the color of the sweater I am considering buying I take it out from under the blue fluorescent light in the back of the shop to the front where there's daylight. To make sure that the signature on the painting is not a forgery I fetch a magnifying glass and look closely at the brushwork. To find out the location of The Gambia I dig out my atlas and scrutinize the map of Africa. To understand what caused the conflict in the family I get the wife's and children's side of the story as well as the husband's. I find Anton Webern's music fascinating but baffling; so I enroll in a course on classical music of the twentieth century in the hope of learning how to listen to it. In short, I employ ways of finding out things, and better ways of finding out things on matters about which I already have views, and ways of gaining awareness of things, and ways of gaining more discriminative awareness of things of which I am already aware. I employ what might be called belief-practices and awareness-practices. We all do. And when we do, we move around bodily in the world and interact with our fellow human beings — all the while intentionally acting upon our environment, including our technological environment, and not just reacting to it. Traditional epistemology — if the characterization which I gave just above is anywhere near correct — has massively neglected to reflect on the belief-practices and awareness-practices in which we all engage.

Neglected such reflection in favor of what? In favor of reflecting, first, on our cognitive *constitution.* What is the *nature* of perception? Does it consist of having mental representations of external objects or do we have direct awareness of objects? What is the *nature* of memory? Those are the sorts of questions asked. And in favor, secondly, of reflecting on the *nature* of knowledge — not on how we go about acquiring knowledge but on its very nature. It is my own conviction that the sterility and stalemates of epistemology are in good measure due to its myopic focus on our cognitive constitution at the expense of reflecting on the practices whereby that constitution is employed. But I'm not going to argue that case here; here it's enough to be aware of both constitution and practices.

In turn, we must learn to think of our cognitive constitution in a much more nuanced way than is customary. I can best make the point I want to make here by using a certain aspect of the workings of computers as a model for thinking about the doxastic side of our lives. We as human beings are all dispositionally hard-wired in such a way that, upon such-and-such things happening to us, we become aware of such-and-such entities; and upon becoming aware of such-and-such entities, we believe thus-and-so. In addition, we are all dispositionally hard-wired in such a way that upon such-and-such things happening to us, we acquire new awareness-dispositions and new belief-dispositions.

But in addition to being hard-wired in this way, each of us is also programmed in a certain way. And whereas the hard-wiring is remarkably similar from person to person, the way we are programmed differs wildly from person to person — and indeed, from time to time within a given person's life. Depending on how one is programmed, a given input will or will not yield a certain awareness, and a certain awareness will or will not yield a certain belief. Most of the time my programming is such that if I perceive a chair in good light, the belief will be formed in me, immediately and ineluctably, that I'm perceiving a chair and that there's a chair before me. But if, on a given occasion of perceiving a chair, my programming includes the firm belief that right then and there I am looking at a very skillfully painted *trompe l'oeil* stage design, then the belief will not be forthcoming in me that I am perceiving a chair and that there's a chair before me. Nor would those beliefs be forthcoming in me, upon perceiving a chair, if I lacked the concept of a chair.

How do we acquire our cognitive programming? We acquire it by way of the output of our already programmed constitution becoming components of our new program. Which beliefs will be formed in us by a given input is almost never a function just of the input to our dispositional nature coupled with the concepts we possess and our attentiveness at the moment. Almost always, beliefs we already have function as elements of our programming. And those beliefs were the output of earlier operations of our programmed constitution. In that way, we function *inside* our system of beliefs. Inside our constitution too. Inside our doxastically programmed constitution. We use beliefs to form beliefs, and then use those latter to form yet others. Lest there be misunderstanding, let me add that much of our programming is not so much personal as social. We also operate inside a tradition.

And now for a sad but crucial point: many of the beliefs which function as elements of our programming are false, with the consequence that our personal programs at many points don't enable access to reality but obstruct it. Running throughout all our personal programmings are glitches consisting of false beliefs functioning to obstruct the formation of true beliefs — and other such glitches as habits of inattention. Though of course nobody's program is just one big glitch!

To return to the Grand Project of the academy: nobody who has thought about the matter has ever supposed that in the academy one just stares at the truth. All have supposed that to enter the academy is to be inducted into certain practices of awareness and belief — certain ways of conducting one's cognitive constitution. Nobody in the past ever put it quite that way, but surely that's what Plato had in mind when he spoke of the philosopher's employment of dialectics, what Aquinas and Descartes had in mind when they spoke of *scientia,* what Locke had in mind when he outlined his optimal practice. One leaves behind the everyday practices for the new and epistemically superior practices — leaves them behind for one's work in the academy, not for one's life in general. And secondly — this is absolutely crucial — inside the academy one lays aside or circumvents the particularity of one's everyday programming and develops a new and fresh program for the matters at hand, free of all those glitches present in our everyday programmings.

How could one ever do that? How could one circumvent the programming one already has? Supposedly by allowing the cognitive constitution which one shares with all human beings — which one possesses just qua human being — to put one in touch with the relevant facts. "To the things themselves," as Locke put it. One lets one's perceptual capacities put one in touch with external objects. One lets one's reason put one in touch with necessary truths. One lets one's consciousness put one in touch with one's own mental life. And then, by the exercise of reason, one makes valid inferences. In all those at whom we looked — Plato, Aquinas, Descartes, Locke — one finds this picture of beginning with direct awareness of facts and then proceeding by good inference from there. Of starting from that foundation and building the house right this time, as one does not and cannot start from that foundation and build the house right in everyday life. Foundationalism is fundamental to the Grand Project. Particularities will of course emerge. The trained art historian learns things by looking at paintings under a magnifying glass that I now could not learn thus; he has been suitably programmed, I have not. But these particularized programmings are to be ones that emerge within the academy, in the course of starting from the foundation by using our generic constitution. Instead of obstructing access to reality, such grounded particularities enable access.

Something like that is the Grand Project which has inspired the academy of the West. And once we see that that was the project, it's obvious why such particularities as feminism and liberationism — along with masculinism and Occidentalism and all others — have been rejected out of hand. These are particularities which are *brought to* the academy from the everyday rather than emerging within the academy from the superior practices of the academy employed by persons functioning qua generic human beings. They have not been developed from the ground up. And though of course they will exhibit some bit of insight here and there — nobody is totally out of touch with reality — overall they represent bias and prejudice, obstructing rather than enabling access to reality.

The Grand Project has come under relentless attack in recent years, from many directions. I myself think it is pure illusion to suppose that upon entering the academy we can circumvent the programming we have acquired in everyday life and begin afresh by employing our hard-wired, unprogrammed cognitive constitution to gain awareness of certain facts. Locke himself, in a fascinating passage late in his *Essay concerning Human Understanding,* admitted as much, without ever quite realizing that he had done so. The admission occurs in his discussion of why people sometimes go wrong in their employment of the practice he recommends — why they sometimes make "wrong estimates of probability," as he puts it. One illustration that he offers is this: the doctrine of transubstantiation is necessarily false, self-evidently so. Yet a person reared in Catholicism from youth up will not emerge believing it's false, no matter how intently he stares at the doctrine. Instead he will sort through all his other beliefs and eliminate those which seem to him incompatible with the doctrine. And here's another example, this time in Locke's own words:

> Would it not be an insufferable thing for a learned professor, and that which his scarlet would blush at, to have his authority of forty years standing, wrought out of hard rock Greek and Latin, with no small expense of time and candle, and confirmed by general tradition, and a reverend beard, in an instant overturned by an upstart novelist [i.e., deviser of novelties]? Can any one expect that he should be made to confess, that what he taught his scholars thirty years ago, was all error and mistake; and that he sold them hard words and ignorance at a very dear rate.[2]

You see the point. The person reared in Catholicism has been programmed in such a way that grasping the doctrine of transubstantiation does not produce in him what Locke thinks is the right outcome — the belief that the doctrine is necessarily false. And the old professor has been programmed in such a way that when presented with the novel theory of a young scholar which contradicts his own, he fails to see any plausibility in it whatsoever.

The point is general. The image of departing from the everyday and entering the special and better is profoundly misleading. We cannot, upon entering the academy, manage to use just our generic cognitive constitution on the topics of concern to the academician. Whether we like it or not, that particular programming we acquired during our life in the everyday functions as we work within the academy. Without such programming, we couldn't even operate in the academy. Dichotomizing isn't possible. The programming we acquired during our life in the everyday contributes to determining our response not just to the facts

2. John Locke, *An Essay concerning Human Understanding* 4.20.1.

with which we deal in ordinary life but to the facts with which we deal in the academy. What transpires in the academy is not an alternative to everyday life but an intensification and extrapolation of that.

The point could be elaborated. But since it's familiar — though not, indeed, in quite the form I have presented it — I propose to move on to the topic which brings us around to our opening. The particularities of programming — that is, of particular habits of awareness, of particular concepts, of particular beliefs — which we bring with us from everyday life to the academy have traditionally been regarded as biases and prejudices obstructing our access to reality. That is the ground for turning away all particularist perspectival learning at the doorway of the academy. The prevalent current argument for allowing them entrance, on the other hand, is starkly political: it assumes that no one ever has any awareness of reality and argues on that ground that it would be unjustly discriminatory to exclude any perspective. If we are all prisoners in our own houses of interpretation, what justification could there be for preferring one kind of prison to another?

I want to present for consideration an approach very different from either of those. May it not be that certain of the perspectives which belong to our narrative identities give us access to realms of reality which would otherwise be extremely difficult to come by? May it not be that some of them constitute in that way privileged cognitive access? It's true that justice requires admitting forthrightly perspectival learning into the academy. But may it not be that there is another reason as well, one which pertains more directly to what the academy is all about? May it not be that we can expect to learn something from the working out of a feminist perspective on epistemology, something that it's most unlikely the rest of us would ever learn on our own? May it not be that we can expect to learn something from the working out of a liberationist perspective on theology, something that it's most unlikely the rest of us would ever learn on our own? And so forth.

"May it not be?" I asked. That's only to pose a possibility. What about actuality? I must admit that I don't know what to offer here but personal testimony. I have in fact found it illuminating to read some of the writings of those whose narrative identity comprises belonging to the underside of society and who look at the Bible and Christian theology from that particularist perspective. I have in fact found it illuminating to read some of the writings of those whose narrative identity comprises being women and who look at the literature of the Western tradition from that particular perspective. I have in fact found it illuminating to read some of the writings of those whose narrative identity comprises being victims of Western imperialism and who look at history from that perspective. And so on. I don't dispute that much of what has been written from one and another such perspective has been silly — though I am myself not of the view that silliness had to await entrance into the academy until about fifteen years ago when particularist perspectival learning forced its way in. Neither do I dispute that much of what goes into particularist perspectives functions to obscure rather than illuminate. All I insist on is that there's more to it than that. Narrative identities also afford privileged cognitive access. Privileged cognitive access to facts of concern to the academy. Our narrative identities lead us to notice things and believe things which otherwise would almost certainly go unnoticed and unbelieved.

Important implications for the ethos of the academy follow from this way of regarding the emergence of perspectivalism. The academy must be a place where genuine dialogue takes place among the representatives of different perspectives. By genuine dialogue I mean: dialogue characterized by willingness to speak and willingness to listen. The hope of all together beginning from a foundation of facts discerned by the employment of our generic constitution, unprogrammed by any particularities, is a hopeless hope. But if the dying of that hope results in nothing more than a multiplicity of perspectival ghettos within the academy, then woe are we. I have argued that the deep significance for the academy of perspectival learning is that it's characteristic of our narrative identities — of certain of them, not all of them — to give us privileged cognitive access to certain aspects of reality. The academy should be a place where insights of that sort are elicited into consciousness, then articulated and developed. But the ultimate point of such intraperspectival endeavors is that what is discerned and learned be shared with those of us whose narrative identity is different — so that all together we can arrive at a richer and more accurate understanding. Agreement is an asymptotic goal of the academy rather than a secured beginning. But that presupposes that the representatives of each particular perspective are willing both to share their insights with those outside and willing to listen to their critique.

It has already become clear that such an ethos will neither be easily

come by nor easily sustained when achieved. One thing which under-
mines it is *the nursing of resentment.* Now that the hegemony of the
purportedly universal has been lifted and particularisms of many sorts
have found their voice in society and academy, one is startled to learn
how deep resentment goes — women against men, people of color
against whites, the rest of the world against the West, Islam against
Christianity, atheists against religion, gays against straights, Ukrainians
against Russians. The list goes on and on. Genuine dialogue is impossible in the presence of nursed resentment. There has to be forgiveness. But let me add that for the *unrepentant* victimizer to ask forgiveness
from the victim is immoral manipulation.

Even more destructive of the ethos needed for genuine dialogue is
claiming the privilege of silence on the ground of suffering. Nowadays one hears
one group or another insisting that its identity has been shaped by its
suffering, that its suffering has been like unto no other, that those who
have not experienced its suffering can never understand it, and that
consequently dialogue is impossible. For whereas dialogue aims at agreement, its prerequisite is understanding. So what's the point of talking to
the other? We'll talk to ourselves, where dialogue is possible. This, I say,
is what one hears. And there's deep truth in it. Suffering does isolate. Yet
it's possible to go beyond nursing one's suffering to owning it redemptively — at which point one no longer claims it as entitlement to the
privilege of silence, but offers it as strange gift to one's other.

"Forgiveness" and "suffering owned redemptively." I have deliberately
chosen words with Christian connotations. What is needed, if the
academy is to survive in the face of injury and suffering, are those
fundamental acts of the soul taught us by Christ for walking in his Way:
forgiveness, and the redemptive owning of suffering, and repentance on
the part of those who need the forgiveness and caused the suffering. And
beyond those acts of the soul, what is needed, if the academy is to survive
amidst the revenge of the particular, is the embrace of the conviction,
fundamental to Christianity, Judaism, and Islam alike, that there is more
to human beings than the merely particular. There is a shared nature.
Split, indeed, into fallen and destined. About our fallen nature, it's not far
from the truth to say that we seek to gain power over others while eluding
their attempt to gain power over us. But about our destined nature,
something quite different has to be said: in this aspect of our nature we
image God, and by virtue of this aspect of our nature we are entitled to

the attitudes and actions which acknowledge the presence within us of an inalienable and inviolable dignity.

I have been hinting in these last paragraphs that to be a Christian is to have a narrative identity which incorporates a perspective on reality that enables, rather than inhibits, discernment of dimensions of reality. Enables, for example, discernment of the role of forgiveness in life, and of redemptively owned suffering, and of repentance; enables discernment of a human nature split into fallen and destined, with the latter possessing an ineradicable dignity calling for respect. But this only begins to detail the discernment enabled by possessing the narrative identity of being a Christian. The academy must also provide a place for that perspectival learning which is Christian learning — provided that those who practice it not only articulate their own perspective but honor the other by taking the risk of engaging in genuine dialogue.

My argument has been that to understand what is going on in the academy today, we must take note of more than just the play of power in the service of interest. We must discern the loosening of the grip on our imaginations of the Grand Project which has inspired the academy for some twenty-five hundred years. I myself believe that the grip of that project on our imaginations *should* be loosened, and that it should be loosened for a number of reasons. The reason I have chosen to develop on this occasion is that certain of our narrative identities enable, rather than obstruct, access to dimensions of reality. They constitute positions of privileged cognitive access.

In closing, let me come clean and admit that the way of looking at the academy and academic learning for which I have argued does not really go against the *entire* Western tradition. That tradition is not quite as monolithic as I have presented it as being. At bottom what I have argued for is an Augustinian way of looking at the matter. Augustine believed that only if one departs from the condition of generic humanity and adopts that highly particular stance which consists of loving God above all else can one genuinely understand the fundamental structure of reality. Misplaced love and hostility hinder knowledge; loving the truly lovable enables knowledge. I believe he was profoundly right about that.

ELIZABETH KAMARCK MINNICH

If You Want Truth, Work for Justice: Some Reflections on Partiality versus Particularity in Relation to Universality

❦   ❦

FOR OVER THIRTY YEARS, I have been working (always, of course, with many other people) to engage the academy with the efforts of this age of movements for justice. Initially, the engagement we sought focused on justice, not on knowledge. We did our small bit to help organize the Northern Students' Movement to support the struggle for civil rights, for example, but did not question at all whether the virulent racism so starkly evident in segregation had any relation to the knowledge we were being taught. Similarly, when this wave of the women's movement began, even as we explored how "the personal is political," we did not at first ask whether or how knowledge variously premised on assumptions of what it means to be human, which and whose activities are significant enough to be studied, might also be political. And even the teach-ins of the Vietnam War period were additions — or, temporarily as during strikes, substitutions — to "normal" teaching.

Truth as well as justice was also an issue, in the sense that many did come to believe that U.S. citizens had been lied to, given false promises, and misled about the inclusiveness of "the American Dream" and the nature of American "interests" abroad. But what was taught as knowledge worthy of transmission to rising generations of citizens privileged enough to attend colleges and universities was not at first critiqued for its possible implication with the injustices that activated waves of students and teachers. In the mid-1970s, for example, when I was working as an administrator at Barnard College, we planned one of a series of conferences called "The Scholar and the Feminist" at which we were still debating whether, more than how, scholarship could have any relation to the equity issues raised by feminism.

But by then such questions were indeed emerging in differing but, I believe, profoundly related ways from the various movements. Today, we see everywhere their fruits. Considered by some healthy and liberating, by others poisonous and destructive, critiques of the contemporary professionalized academic disciplines and new interdisciplinary fields have proliferated: black studies (now often "African American/African studies"), women's studies, ethnic studies (as umbrella department or in the form of studies of particular groups and traditions), peace studies, environmental studies, critical studies (as a field, and as a branch of fields, e.g., critical legal studies), cultural studies, and more. And scholarship has poured forth from people first creating and then developing all these fields, separately as well as in conversation with each other and, to varying degrees, with intellectual movements such as the European-initiated postmodernism and deconstructionism (which also emerged with justice movements in the late sixties).

During these intellectually turbulent years, my own work has focused on efforts to transform the curriculum to make it more inclusive. I will not here discuss that work, as it is the subject of my book, *Transforming Knowledge*.[1] Suffice it to say, for our purposes here, that it centers on and explores the implications of an understanding to which I came after thousands of conversations with faculty colleagues across the country about their courses. It became clear to me, as I listened and as I followed the new scholarship from all the emerging fields, that something quite obvious — but not easy nevertheless to see clearly and very difficult to change — was going on. Put it this way: like the ducks in Hans Christian Andersen's tale of "The Ugly Duckling," we had come to believe that one 'kind' of human (one kind of fowl in Andersen's story) was the

---

1. Elizabeth Kamarck Minnich, *Transforming Knowledge* (New York: Oxford University Press, 1990).

generic kind, the inclusive kind, the representative and normative and ideal-setting kind. Thus "man" was declared generic, claiming inclusive neutrality as to 'kind,' yet simultaneously moving other 'kinds' (of humans, of fowls) out of the defining category and down the scale of significance and worth. Like the ducks, then, some few of our species judged others not just somewhat in some regards different, but "ugly," lesser, odd, deviant. As a result, "history" was actually the history of a few and did not do justice — or tell the truth — about the vast majority of humankind (women alone being 51 percent of our kind). From the perspective of standards set for ducks, a young swan can only be judged "ugly." From the perspective of European "civilization," other civilizations came to be called "cultures" and adjudged "primitive," "irrational," "undeveloped."

A part, that is, had been defined as the whole, which left no room for the rest of us except as exceptions, deviants, aberrations — lesser creatures moved out of the inclusive category and down the scale of "human" (but actually only partially defined) worth. It is no surprise, then, that some still see all the new and retrieved scholarship of, by, and about all those for so long devalued as "lowering standards." If the standards are defined by the few who believed all women and whole groups of men ought not to be educated or studied, that is unavoidable — but it is hardly adequate or accurate. And it continues to work to legitimate injustices even as it distorts our efforts at knowledge, at truth and meaning, that is not premised on the confusion of parts with the whole.

Thus, my title: "If You Want Truth, Work for Justice." Without the propaedeutic of a commitment to justice, scholarship is very likely indeed to emerge skewed along the lines of beliefs that created and perpetuate and justify injustice. If we wish to honor the promise of scholarship to be impartial and disinterested, we must hold it to its own values — just as we have been holding the United States to its principle that "all men are created equal," finding here the basis of an inclusiveness not originally intended.

With that background, let me then turn to our present topic, the relation of religions and theologies to today's emergent critiques and reconfigurations of knowledge, hence also of education. I bring a particular perspective to this effort, so of course I must acknowledge and characterize it. Being very careful to locate ourselves is one of the measures we can take in times in which what once passed as general, even universal, can no longer be assumed to live up to its own claims.

I have recently begun to ask myself the question of why issues of religion have not come up for me in the contexts of my work in all these years, a question that separates itself into three strands I can honestly address. The first strand is personal: why have I not related my work to religious considerations? The second has to do with the work: why has it not pressed me to explore its connections to religion? The third concerns those with whom I have done the work: why have I not through them more often encountered religion as a helpful or problematic or relevant issue?

I ask these questions not just to locate myself and my work but also because I am inclined to agree with Tillich that the answers religion gives must be answers to authentic questions people have, cast in the terms of their own spirits and hearts, and in the language of their times. The responses of religion will be, in Tillich's location of religion, to the "deepest" aspects of those questions, to the levels at which they connect the universal and transcendent to the individual, a connection that should respond authentically to the historically mediated but not reduced-to-history individual. The individual's part in this conversation is, as I see it now, to pay close attention to what her or his questions are, and to see those questions as individual or personal; as configured within, and of, particular times and contexts; and as pressed beyond those particularities by the aspirations of morality to recognize claims both of particularity and of horizons of meaning that cannot be captured by any one formulation, as justice is never captured in any particular act of legislation or historically mediated legal system.

I am undertaking my task in this way, I should also say, because *relationality* is a central concept, issue, and enactment of my work as of my life, so it is always important that I explore not only lines but webs of connections and interactions. Why, then, have I not connected my work on transforming the curriculum to religion? In no small part, my response must begin with the fact that I was not brought up within any one religious community. No particular religion is for me an intimate part of the fabric of my world — not substance of my formative memories, not source of strength and hope and meaning, and not, either, source of searing questions. My parents are the children of Polish Catholic peasants, Russian Jewish intellectuals (the women denied higher education, the men very active in the few spheres open to Jews in Russia), and British Protestants long settled in Virginia. My forebears were enabled in this country to meet, love each other, marry, and have children in part because they all adopted when they arrived here what I can only call Enlightenment values. They shared, that is, aspirations to be above all "rational," and to put that rationality — developed through as much education for the males as possible — to the service of supposedly universalized principles of justice. Let me make that a bit more vivid for you by telling you that my father and my grandfather before him became international economists because they were dedicated to using the wisdom of modern science to alleviate the human suffering and inequity caused by poverty.

Now, you and I know that poverty has not been eradicated, and we also know that it is hard today to place the kind of trust in the social sciences to save the world that many in the dominant European tradition did not so long ago. There has been what I can only call a loss of faith in salvation through science. I do not believe I ever came close to sharing my economist forebears' faith, but I have my own version of the kinds of questions people have when early faith hits later "real life" problems. Having grown up with a familial faith in reason, it is reason's failures that I am most alert to, most critical of, and most desirous of ameliorating through a quest for a more capacious, more complex, more nuanced understanding of our abilities as thinking, speaking, feeling, intuiting, symbol-making, signifying, loving creatures.

Thus, for all these years I have engaged in critique not of religion but of framings of reason and knowledge, of what I have called "the dominant meaning system" as it informs and is perpetuated by the curriculum of higher education — because I also grew up valuing mightily the promise of such education for all people. I want us to do better what we claim to be doing. I want us not to pass on uncritiqued knowledge developed when those who alone were allowed to be educated and who continued to create and legitimate knowledge believed with the dominant culture that only a few 'kinds' of humans were capable of 'proper' reason and so ought to have higher education. "Man who is rational" had, then, to be both "man" and "rational" in ways not discerned from comprehensive consideration of human gifts and potentials but in contradistinction to feminized and racialized ways of thinking and being. We have all lost and suffered too much by such exclusions. How can we "reason together" when reasoning itself has been defined not as the best and fullest of human capacities for knowledge and communication, but as a particular set of intellectualized skills to be developed and used by an oppositionally defined few being prepared to reason for all the others who were to serve and obey them in their role as "head" of household, "head" of faith communities, "head" of state, and "master" of nature and all creation?

More recently, still in conversation with many others across the nation, I have been exploring the critiques and fruitful scholarship of many of the newer, interdisciplinary fields that are now to be found on most of our campuses. In a paper I am now writing for the Association of American Colleges and Universities as part of a national project on the relations among diversity, democracy, and liberal education, I have noted the following as issues most of us are willing to say are important, even critical, to be addressed in our quest as a nation for both truth and justice:

Issues of *inclusion/exclusion* of 'kinds' of people, as citizens and as learners, teachers, and subjects in liberal education; issues of the *relations* among individuals, communities, societies, cultures, and polities taught about and practiced in education; issues of the historical, social, cultural, and political *contexts* of knowledge creation and preservation; (and) issues of how we may, and why we should, search for more inclusive and equitable *common grounds*.

Those of us who work on these issues bring to that work serious moral concerns. As I have said, it was concern for justice — a moral and political concern about human relationality — that led us to question knowledge and education. But when I ask myself to characterize the kinds of Tillichian "deep" questions that could reveal religious implications, I find myself thinking that it is not their deepest roots in faith that are for me at issue, but how all faiths, including 'faith' in reason, have been expressed in human constructs that have historically contradicted their own highest aspirations. It is not, then, universals that trouble me. It is their deformation into partialities, into invidiously ranked 'kinds,' that concerns me. Those partialities make it difficult indeed for any of us to approach with reverently radical openness the mysteries of particularity and of universality.

But as many scholar-activists have worked to undo those blocking partialities, others have responded with concerns about loss and with anger akin to the anger of people defending their faith — confusing, so it seems to me, historically mediated forms with what they are intended to be forms of. Clearly, at one time some of us could believe that being a knowledge worker in the academy was a good thing to be on the face of it. Theories and facts are not practices of justice, it was thought, but they are nevertheless important to it as the disinterested to the interested, the objective to the "merely" subjective, the public to the private, the enduring to the contingent. But now all of those assumptions have been challenged from within and without the academy, and we are faced with a decentering loss of certainty, both intellectual and moral.

Some others are feeling, on the contrary, liberated. A different story of education reveals itself when one takes the stance of one of the excluded while maintaining a sense of self that does not accept one's subsumption into a 'kind' of human whose natural and necessary inferiority, or prescribed specialized function (e.g., labor, productive and/or reproductive), precludes the 'higher' activities of "the life of the mind." Then we see institutions of higher education serving the power and authority hierarchies of unjust orders in untruthful, highly partial ways.

So, where some become defensive in the face of challenges to their faith in the goodness of the life of the mind as it has been defined, others have been animated by those challenges to hope that now a far larger and more diverse "we" can engage questions of the relations of knowledge, meaningfulness, and justice, questions of the relation of the universal, transcendent, timeless to the particular, and of these to the mediating (or blocking) terms of partial historical and cultural formations.

There are here aspects of what have been called "culture wars," and in a sense that is apt. We are indeed struggling over the legitimacy, and sources of legitimation, of culture (on a general and on specific levels) as both matrix of meanings for all (e.g., in the anthropological sense) and as a congeries of particular kinds of activities and products (e.g., "high" culture). But I see no virtue in using military metaphors for our engagement with some of the more interesting and important questions we all face. In fact, I see the tendency to indicate how important something is by using war metaphors and terms as one of the partialities that distort our quests for both truth and justice. For example, I think that my own field, philosophy, would do a lot better in its pursuit of wisdom if we could give up the (need I note, highly gendered) quest for "impregnable" arguments, for positions we can "defend" against all "attackers." I'd prefer pregnant positions developed from fruitful conversations among differing people that give birth to new possibilities, and welcoming postures that invite others into such creative conversations. Similarly for discussions of culture, of truth and meaning and justice and faith: surely we need the best from all of us creatively synthesized, not for one side once again to "win" in ways that deny that side as well as all the rest of us the wisdom of those "defeated." How sad that the "attack/defense" mode of reasoning is still seen as reasoning itself, but commonly it is. When one questions it, one is seen as attacking all possibility of rationality.

Nevertheless, I understand the intensity that is evoked by questioning established definitions. These are issues with roots deep enough to be faithlike, and academics in prevailing systems are no more above various forms of violence than are religious adherents — witness the Crusades and the colonial conquests of Enlightenment times. But surely we aspire to be better.

It would seem, then, that the academy, having been challenged as to its self-justifying self-sufficiency with regard to truth, meaningfulness, and justice, *should* move forward to take up hard and important questions concerning both politics and religion (the two areas most notably banned from the secular ivory tower). Both have indeed done so, but politics much more so than religion, at least in my experience. This is odd: when assumptions of what it means for all and for each of us to be human and in relation with each other — which is, as I keep variously suggesting, what I see as at issue across all the other issues — are brought forward to be questioned, one would think that religions and theologies, in particular, would be prominent in the discussion. But while differing political theories are indeed often invoked, as are differing philosophical framings, theologies are rarely explicitly adduced.

It seems to me that what I have been hearing may not have engaged theological wisdom even on questions for which one would expect it to be illuminating, such as the pressing questions of the relation of the particular to the universal, and of truth to justice, for several reasons.

First, there is of course the history of secularization of the academy that made even the inclusion of religious studies a contentious issue not so long ago. But today, I think theologies have not adequately been drawn on, or religions invoked, more specifically for two other reasons.

The first, and most obvious, is that too many of us have experiences (or, as in my case, come from families whose immigrant forebears had experiences) with religions as being dangerously divisive, in ways ranging all the way from social intolerance to genocide. That is why this country is founded on a separation of church and state, and it is related to the secularization of institutions of higher learning as well. We forget at our peril, I fear, the histories that led to secularization of institutions in a country promising freedom of conscience, whatever distinctions we may draw between faith traditions and the actual practices of some of those who claim them. But, remembering history, we could still benefit from the wisdom of theologies that have emerged from millennia of struggles with just these issues, with the relations between the universal and the particular, with the problems of fallible people in particular situations and times and cultures, with tensions between principles and practices, reason and will and emotion.

The second reason, which is related to the first, comes up more frequently in these particular historical times, I think. It has to do with realizations such as mine that some 'kinds' of people have been defined, and prescribed for, and treated as, unequal, less than fully and properly human in a system in which only a few men were taken to be "man who is rational." What I mean to emphasize by that now is that the devalued 'kinds' of people were then kept from having the kind of *public* life humans require to have a sense of identity and meaningfulness, but that was withheld from supposedly less rational females and some 'kinds' of males. What we are struggling for can be seen, in this view, as the right to emerge from privatized lives, to be seen, heard, recognized, and not only as we are captured and delimited by the definitions of others who have held the power of definition, but as we, in the free, equalized company of many others, may come to define ourselves.

Let me be clear about what is being rebelled against, so I can clarify what the rebellion may be for, and so perhaps why it has focused so on politics and has not, for many of us, led to religious or theological concerns. Being privatized does not mean having a personal life but no public life. Being privatized means being subject, as the law professor

Patricia Williams puts it, to constant and uncontrollable invasion, with no recourse. It means, in fact, having no private life at all. Consider: Africans brought to this country to be enslaved, to be made property, were, in being unjustly, immorally, and untruthfully defined as creatures who could not rightly have rights and so could not be involved in any way in public life, denied private lives as well. One can hardly read any slave narrative without immediately recognizing how thoroughly that was the case.

Nonenslaved women were also long denied private lives by being domesticated, i.e., defined as properly denizens only of the private sphere. Having no public life meant no protected private life for us, either. There were until very recently indeed no laws, no concepts, of marital rape, as an emblematic example, because upon marrying a woman became civically dead, a provision of a man's household, and he could no more be said to have raped her than he could be said to have violated fields he owned when he planted them. He had the legal right to "husband" what was legally his.

To those of us whose deepest values are offended by such assignments of some people to be means for the ends of others, our questions, our passions, have been directed first toward constructions of the political, the public. As I have said, we began with justice concerns. We were pressed by them to critiques of knowledge as we observed their mutual implication — and some of us were also, then, pressed to critique religions and some theologies on the same grounds. Both education and religions became, as some say today, sites of contestation. But even as they did, achieving public personhood, becoming fully part of the creation of equalized political common ground, now seems, to many of us, the basic necessity. When we had no protected public life, our objections to injustices of all kinds were futile. Having no rights, we could ask only for favors, for the "kind condescension" of those with the power to grant or withhold.

And some of us, having focused on de-privatizing and so on the equal rights that protect both private and public lives, have, when we have turned our eyes to faith issues, found ourselves struck by the devaluation of public life that is a part of some faith traditions and that helped discourage many of us from becoming political. It is possible, indeed, to see a relation between our own devaluation and the devaluation of the political and the social. The 'things' of this world that marked its fallen state in contrast to higher values included so many of us, and qualities ascribed to us: the 'higher' was transcendent to our immanent, rational and spiritual to our flesh and passions, independent to our dependency, adult to our childishness, civilized to our primitive. Thus we have come to think we must work not only to de-privatize ourselves and all that was privatized with us, but also to redefine and revalue the public, the political. We insist, then, that knowledge as well as religion is always political, and should be so in ways held accountable as politics should be to the propaedeutic of justice. This discredits none of these human activities: quite the contrary. It calls them on their best aspirations, asking them to rid themselves of old devaluations and discrimination by 'kind.' However, these related efforts get us branded "political" in ways the branders think discredit us for the very same reasons we think we need to revalue the political: because it has been taken to be "bad" or at least lesser to be political, and especially so for those of us who were privatized.

Our disruptive questioning seems to transgress, then, some definitional and evaluative hierarchical boundaries and so has not easily been engaged with by those to whom it has seemed, as I have said, too political. It has also seemed, in its questioning of some hierarchical framings and valuations, too "relativistic." But while I accept even as I revalue the charge that we are "political," I do not think we are all *relativists* in our refusal of hierarchical systems premised on invidiously ranked and oppositionally defined 'kinds' of humans and aspects of human lives. We are, I think, *relationalists.* Our questions are questions about justice as it has served, and injustice as it has distorted, relations and relationality. For an example from my own limited store, I think of Buber when I focus on how we are to reframe understandings of relationality grounded in public, political equality firmly enough to look beyond it to its own grounds on a transcendent level. What Buber famously called "I-It" thinking is precisely about distortions in relations and practices, and surely, to become able to achieve "I-Thou" mutually respectful, relational being is a goal many of us can share.

But to do so honestly, without once again sliding some 'kinds' of us back out of the publicly recognized *and so also* protected-in-private equality for which we are still struggling, we continue to need to critique our thinking and our languages in *all* of our worlds of meaning and action. For that effort, it does not suffice to dream of "oneness," of "unity," of "common ground," of "universal values" while conflating those mysteries with historically invidious, partial forms.

I return, then, to higher education as an example now of a kind of work in which I think all of us need to engage in our various spheres. None of us has "it" right; none of us is all wrong. Religions and theologies have as much to contribute as they do to learn about how we are to transform the partialities that still entrap us.

For example, in 1852, John Henry Cardinal Newman began his inaugural discourses as rector of the new Catholic University of Ireland with what we know today as the highly influential book, *The Idea of a University*.[2] Newman recognized, as we also are called to recognize, that education is indeed related, and should respond, to past injustices. As Jaroslav Pelikan wrote in 1992, in *The Idea of the University: A Reexamination,* "What was called for (in Newman's times) was a university that would help make reparations for these crimes" — characterized by Newman as being "the wrongs of the oppressed" among "nationalities" that "are waking into life" — "on behalf not only of the Irish but of all the oppressed and underdeveloped 'nationalities' and peoples of the earth." Seeking thus to respond to and transcend an unjust past, Newman gave voice to his dreams of a universal university. He wrote, "I see a flourishing university. . . . Thither, as to a sacred soil, the home of their fathers, and the fountain-head of their Christianity, students are flocking from East, West, and South, from America and Australia and India, from Egypt and Asia Minor, with the ease and rapidity of a locomotion not yet discovered . . . all speaking one tongue, all owning one faith, all eager for one large true wisdom; and thence, when their stay is over, going back again to carry over all the earth 'peace to men of good will.' "[3]

I admire Newman's work, yet I cannot embrace it as meeting my own desires for justice and inclusion in education. I hear too loudly that "one tongue," that "one faith," that is to be carried "over all the earth." I do not believe that equality requires that we all join together to be the same in any one group's terms, even as I fully recognize what progress it was for Newman as for others to come to believe that some 'kinds' of us were even capable of such sameness.

2. John Newman, *The Idea of a University* (Oxford: Oxford University Press, 1976).
3. Jaroslav Pelikan, *The Idea of the University: A Reexamination* (New Haven: Yale University Press, 1992), p. 147.

I value more the wisdom of other voices, such as that of the great African American educator Anna Julia Cooper, who wrote in 1892:

> It is not the intelligent woman vs. the ignorant woman, nor the white woman vs. the black, the brown, and the red. . . . It is not even the cause of woman vs. man. Nay, 'tis woman's strongest vindication for speaking that the world needs to hear her voice. . . . The world has had to limp along with the wobbling gait and the one-sided hesitancy of a man with one eye. Suddenly the bandage is removed from the other eye and the whole body is filled with light. It sees a circle where before it saw a segment. The darkened eye restored, every member rejoices with it.[4]

This sounds to me more nearly honoring of a universal vision than Newman in that it does not confuse sameness with equality, and so it is capable of a capacious vision of wholeness that does not conflate it with any part but works organically with all. And then I hear a spokesperson for multiculturalism, Ron Takaki, writing in 1993 to remind us of something we ought not to need reminding of: "The signs of America's ethnic diversity can be discerned across the continent. . . . Many diverse ethnic groups have contributed to the building of the American economy. . . . They worked in the South's cotton fields, New England's textile mills, Hawaii's canefields, New York's garment factories, California's orchards, Washington's salmon canneries, and Arizona's copper mines. . . . Seeking to know how they fit into America, many young people have become listeners: they are eager to learn about the hardships and humiliations experienced by their parents and grandparents. They want to hear their stories, unwilling to remain ignorant or ashamed of their identity and past." And then Takaki says, "The telling of stories liberates. . . . Native-American novelist Leslie Marmon Silko cautioned: I will tell you something about stories. . . . They aren't just entertainment. Don't be fooled."[5]

This, too, I hear as animated by a sense of a universal moral horizon

4. Anna Julia Cooper, *A Voice from the South* (Oxford: Oxford University Press, 1988), pp. 121-23.

5. Ronald Takaki, *A Different Mirror: A History of Multicultural America* (Boston: Little, Brown, 1993), pp. 12, 15.

that comprehends many more particular viewpoints, more stories, differing modes of reasoning, teaching, learning than have been included. Takaki is not saying, "Ours, not yours." He is saying, "All of us, not only some." Neither he nor Cooper is trying to close us away from each other, to divide or to homogenize us. On the contrary, both ask us to open to each other through recognition of our profound mutual relationality, our differences that make us all so much more than any part of us can ever be.

J. Wesley Brown has written, "Education is a process of human development. Liberal education makes one aware of the social, historical, and cultural factors that have affected that development," not to reduce knowledge of them, but on the contrary precisely to keep it from being trapped within them. We cannot overcome what we refuse even to acknowledge. Brown continues, "[C]oncerned for a more complete understanding of the human condition, we who have been schooled in the classic forms of Western thought need to turn the critical skills we have acquired back upon our own tradition to see whose interests and values have been served and perpetuated in that tradition. . . . If practitioners of the liberal arts fail to take up this task we acquiesce to the forms of human exploitation that rely on ignorance and unquestioned tradition in order to perpetuate their power." And he concludes, not by saying there is nothing left but a relativistic contestation of power, as some postmodernists might say and as many of us are wrongly charged with holding, but by saying, "Study of the liberal arts bears a moral imperative; the quest for Truth is not a disinterested quest. The interest which informs this quest is commitment to a more inclusive vision of what it means to be human, and of how humankind may live together on the earth."[6]

This sounds to me like a vision of education compatible with a similarly critiqued theology, such as that limned by theologian Rosemary Ruether. Ruether writes that

> The feminist religious revolution thus promises to be more radical and far-reaching (than other "liberationist" theologies). . . . It goes behind the symbolic universe that has been constructed by patriarchal

6. J. Wesley Brown, from an unpublished statement written for Saint Olaf College, Minnesota.

civilization, both in its religious and in its modern secular forms. It reaches forward to an alternative that can heal the splits between 'masculine' and 'feminine,' between mind and body, between males and females as gender groups, between society and nature, and between races and classes.[7]

I do not hear Cooper, or Takaki, or Silko, or Brown, or Ruether as relativistic, as I have said, nor as destructive of universals. Hardly: their visions yearn toward "healing," transcending, moving behind historically framed divisions to find their deeper grounds in wholeness. What their positions are indeed destructive of is universals cast in partial terms that thus contradict themselves at the root. I do, however, hear in what they propose an embracing of some meanings of the term "particularism," in two ways with which I agree. First, they remind us that there are groups of people on whom those who would know must focus in order to undo the ignorance willed to us by hierarchies of 'kinds.' One must not, after all, continue to generalize from too small a sample. Second, they also remind us that particular stances, voices, narratives, sets of beliefs can signify universals — and that those particular stances belong to no predetermined group or 'kind' of us.

Both of those points seem to me unproblematic, but I recognize that I am in the vicinity here of today's absolutized attacks on all and any universals, with which I do not agree. I cannot help but object, for example, when some postmodernist feminists attack as "essentialist" those who attempt, finally and at long last publicly, to speak "as women," or when they call on women to "speak" — or write — "the body," as if this were not what we have always been supposed, in unjust systems, to do. I am suspicious of absolutized attacks on absolutism: too often, all they do is reverse what was, thereby actually changing very little.

As Susan Bordo puts it:

Deconstructionism answers (the question of how the human knower is to 'know' a destabilized world) with constant vigilant suspicion of all determinate readings of culture and a partner aesthetic of ceaseless

7. Rosemary Radford Ruether, *Women-Church: Theology and Practice* (San Francisco: Harper & Row, 1985), p. 3.

textual play as an alternative ideal. Here is where deconstructionism may slip into its own fantasy of escape from human locatedness — by supposing that the critic can become wholly protean by adopting endlessly shifting, seemingly inexhaustible vantage points, none of which are 'owned' by either the critic or the author of a text under examination. . . . But, I would argue, the philosopher's fantasy of transcendence has not yet been abandoned. The historical specifics of the modernist, Cartesian version have simply been replaced with a new postmodern configuration of detachment, a new imagination of disembodiment: a dream of being *everywhere*.[8]

I agree. Bordo, however, appears here to be preparing to argue for a view of "locatedness" that has no connection to transcendence, wherever that transcendence may 'be.' But can we not focus on locatedness precisely so as not to confuse it with transcendence? Those of us who do not wish to turn things upside down one more time, who want to get rid of mistakes without throwing out aspirations, find ourselves caught between the Scylla of charges that we are being far too divisive and relativist and in an absolutized sense particularist, and the Charybdis of charges that we are being essentialist, or universalist. We are pressed to choose among a scientistic, Enlightenment rationalist view that claims to be from nowhere (but was foundationally defined from and for a very specific somewhere); some religions that conflate their historically shaped formulations of particularity with the mysteries of both particularity and the universal itself; and a postmodern view that is supposed to be from everywhere (as if that did not slide into a differently mystified universality). None of these seems particularly inviting, or safe, to me, and I confess that all seem to me tainted by the hubris of belief that humans can ever be certain that we have got it right.

Whether the truths that we yearn for are truths that respond to questions of reason or of faith or of multiple plays of power, as in some postmodernist views, then, I still want to say, "If you want truth, work for justice." Here I am a pragmatist — not an antireligious position, recalling William James, and a highly contemporary position, as in the work of today's most prominent preacher-pragmatist, Cornel West. For

8. Susan Bordo, *The Flight of Objectivity: Essays on Cartesianism and Culture* (Albany: State University of New York Press, 1987).

humans, I want to say with James, there is no difference anywhere that does not make a difference somewhere: show me what you do in this world with others, and I will know what you mean by your faith, whether it be in science, in some kind of philosophical reasoning, in religion, in postmodernism, or whatever.

I see the work of critiquing and transforming the curriculum as part of an ongoing effort of humankind to carry out what that syncretistic thinker and believer, Mohandas Gandhi, called "experiments in truth" in order to remind himself and others that humans do not 'have' Truth. For the present, my work as I have shared in it with many others has consisted of critiquing what I see working in the world as that oxymoron, partial universals. Critiquing intellectual claims to universality (and more modest claims to generality) according to their own claims to be inclusive is one aspect of our work, as is critiquing practices within traditions as to whether they do or do not honor the values of those claims in their dealings with particulars. Thus, for example, when a field of knowledge claims to be inclusive (not of course because it 'contains' all but because it is based on disinterested rather than biased research), we check to see whether that was indeed the case. Similarly, when a faith tradition claims to be on its 'highest' or 'deepest' levels unimplicated with historical constructions of gender, race, or class, we critique its formulations and practices against its own claims thus to have transcended unjust partialities. Few, need I say, emerge as consistently and in all regards true to their own highest aspirations. Nearly all teach us a great deal about both reason and faith-inspired efforts to be so.

Directly related to this kind of critique and of openness to learning from all is the work of bringing forward our own and other located, particular voices, stories, perspectives, experiences that we must all now learn to hear *also* as possibly related to horizons of universal meanings. In a kind of dialectical movement between such particularities and what I call, with Kant, regulative ideas (or in my own language, aspirational ideals) — i.e., ideas and ideals that we can think, and believe, but never fully know — I place my hope for more justly inclusive human systems by which to regulate our lives in this highly particular world in which we must get on with the business of living, loving, and seeking our way together. I have no doubt but that changes we make, assertions we fiercely state, are themselves flawed. They, too, will be human, all too human. But that conviction does not release me from responsibility to take positions and work for changes. Rather, it reminds me to do so as a nonpossessive lover of wisdom, an educator open to learning with and from all students and colleagues, and a citizen in a democracy that has never been monocultural or of only one religious faith.

Listen, then, to one more vision of a kind of education that captures a great deal of what I, with Maxine Greene, believe in, and that I, at least, hope to come to understand better as I continue my work:

> Democracy, Dewey wrote, is a community always in the making. If educators hold this in mind, they will remember that democracy is forever incomplete: it is founded in possibilities. Even in the small, the local spaces in which teaching is done, educators may begin creating the kinds of situations where, at the very least, students will begin telling the stories of what they are seeking, what they know and might not yet know, exchanging stories with others grounded in other landscapes, at once bringing something into being that is in-between. . . . It is at moments like these that persons begin to recognize each other and, in the experience of recognition, feel the need to take responsibility for each other.[9]

Thus can we be both located and open, different but relational, in a small but public space framed beyond its walls by a moral horizon no one of us alone 'knows' in its fullness.

9. Maxine Greene, "Diversity and Inclusion: Toward a Curriculum for Human Beings," *Teachers College Record* 95, no. 2: 211-21.

JEAN HAMPTON

Feminism, Moral Objectivity, and Christianity

THE PHRASE "CULTURE WARS" is a good term to describe the character of life in American universities today — especially because the term "war" is in the plural. It has been a hallmark of my career in academia that I have been involved in not one but many wars. In this essay I want to explain and defend the stands I have taken in these wars, which will involve, in part, explaining how my Christianity is deeply connected not only to those stands, but also to my conviction that I have to continue to fight.

But should we be "fighting" in academia? While it is a fact that warring exists in academia, we should ask, from a normative point of view, whether this is a good thing for the academy. I shall argue that it all depends upon the kind of "war" one is talking about. There is more than one way to wage a war of ideas. Indeed, perhaps even more important than the substantive view for which any of us fights is the way we conduct the fight. So I don't lament all "warring" in academia — only a certain kind of "warring" that is mean-minded and shuts down thought. To the extent that this bad kind of warring persists in academic life, it will be unpleasant, unproductive, and poisonous to the intellectual life of this country. We need a way to disagree with one another, a way to press our arguments and ideas, that is both morally permissible and healthy for the intellectual life of the academy. I shall attempt to define such a method of disagreement: it is characterized by respect for one's opponents and a commitment to reasoning with them. I am tempted to call it "combat between friends" as a way of insisting that this method is committed both to respecting others *and* to disagreeing with them (so that respect isn't the same as being "nice and agreeable"). I shall maintain that if our disagreements are conducted in this fashion, in terms that honor and appeal to the reason of those with whom we disagree, they will represent intellectual engagement and interaction of the very best kind.

I. Fights with the Naturalists

One war I have actively been involved in is with a group that I will call "the naturalists." Naturalism is a metaphysical position that is committed to the view that the only sound way to understand the world is to use the methods of science. One might say that naturalists "worship" science. Note that naturalists needn't be scientists, and indeed, scientists needn't be naturalists (so, e.g., any religious scientist would not count as a naturalist). Naturalists disparage superstition, astrology, magic using, religion, and moral objectivism. Such things, say the naturalists, are all of a piece, insofar as they rely on modes of thinking that are outmoded remnants of failed approaches to dealing with the world, whose claim to authority science not only destroys but implicitly ridicules. To quote Frank Ramsey, a brilliant logician, philosopher, and mathematician who wrote in the 1920s: "Theology and Absolute Ethics are two famous subjects which we have realized have no real objects."[1]

Naturalists do not renounce objectivity: instead they invoke the objectivity that they take theoretical reason to provide. Science, when it is well conducted, is supposed to involve practices and methods that perfectly realize the requirements of reason. Philosophers who are naturalists mix philosophical reflection with scientific theorizing and data from experimentation — in psychology, economics, biology, or physics — thereby lending to their philosophical theories the authoritative aura of the master discipline.

---

1. Frank Ramsey, "There Is Nothing to Discuss," epilogue in *Foundations of Mathematics,* ed. R. B. Braithwaite (New York: Harcourt Brace, 1931), pp. 291-92.

For anyone who is a moral objectivist or a Christian, this position must be fought — in order to make room for a reality that naturalists, through their assumptions and methods, are committed to denying. But how is that fight to be conducted?

Some Christians I know in the academy have decided not to fight at all. They worship privately and philosophize publicly in a way that is respectful of science, albeit not worshipful of it. Their respect is, in my view, legitimate. Yet not to stand up for a moral and religious reality that one believes in is a kind of quiet betrayal of those realities. So in my view one has to stand up for that reality. How does one do it, and do it effectively?

There are two ways that I believe are effective. The first way is to point out the extent to which science itself betrays its own values and is informed by thinking and ideas that are not rationally legitimate. There is some interesting literature that makes this point, and the most interesting is, in my view, found in feminist writings. For example, feminists have done some critical studies of both the history of biology and of current biological theories, showing the extent to which sexist ideology has played, and continues to play, a powerful role in the construction of biological theories.[2] Consider one feminist's review of some of the assumptions of nineteenth-century biology:

Nineteenth century biologists and physicians claimed that women's brains were smaller than men's and that women's ovaries and uteruses required much energy and rest in order to function properly. They "proved" that therefore young girls must be kept away from schools and college once they begin to menstruate and warned that without this kind of care women's uteruses and ovaries will shrivel and the human race die out. Yet again, this analysis was not carried over to poor women, who were not only required to work hard, but often were said to reproduce *too* much. Indeed, scientists interpreted the fact that poor women could work hard and yet bear many children as a sign that they were more animal-like and less highly evolved than upper class women.[3]

2. For a variety of essays that pursue this theme, see Nancy Tuana, ed., *Feminism and Science* (Bloomington: Indiana University Press, 1989).

3. Ruth Hubbard, "Science, Facts and Feminism," in *Feminism and Science*, p. 123.

The ludicrous nature of these biologists' conclusions only underscores the point that unjust social structures can be a powerful influence on the content of scientific theories. The aura of science, if feminist scientists such as Ruth Hubbard are right, does not come in any pure and unadulterated sense from the authority of reason alone but reflects the power structures of the societies in which these theories are developed. That the feminist critique is virtually undeniable in the face of the evidence helps us to see a way to break the hold that science has over many minds, and to get people to think anew about the extent to which science can be used to pronounce upon the reality of gods and goods.

This feminist critique has two forms, one naive and one sophisticated. The naive criticism presupposes that, having identified the prejudice or bias in a scientific discipline, the remedy is simply to erase the bias, leaving a theory that is now pure and completely reason-driven. The more sophisticated critique takes the task of "fixing" science to be much harder, insofar as the concepts, metaphors, strategies, and forms of experimentation in a science can be deeply influenced by the society out of which the science grows, so that, if the society is infested with injustice, so too is the science. If this is right, making science pure of injustice is much harder than simply getting out an eraser and deleting certain lines in the theory: it may well involve reconstructing the theory from its roots. As Hubbard puts it, to do science well, we must "watch ourselves push the bus in which we are riding."[4] But notice that even the sophisticated critique of science holds out the ideal of a science based on reason alone, in search of truth and free of truth-obfuscating features that prejudiced researchers now bring to their theories.

The second way to undermine naturalism involves not merely weakening science's de facto authority but also defending the authority of morality and religion. And the way to do this is, once again, to rely on reason. For reason is what these naturalists celebrate and it is the basis for any criticism of science that they will respect — that is, to the extent that a scientific theory loses its grounding in reason and allows bias, prejudice, and emotional commitments to influence the content of its theorizing, to that extent the naturalists themselves are committed to rejecting that theory. Hence, using reason to develop arguments for

4. Ruth Hubbard, "Have Only Men Evolved?" in *Discovering Reality*, ed. Sandra Harding and Merrill Hintikka (Dordrecht, Netherlands: D. Reidel, 1983), p. 66.

moral objectivism and certain religious tenets is a way to get a naturalist who is deeply committed to reason to listen to these arguments. Indeed, in my experience naturalists actually *will* listen to them, in ways that result in minds getting changed and new ideas getting formed. I must say that I take many of these naturalists to be the best of my opponents — indeed, many of them are my good friends. The struggles we have are usually conducted in terms that are friendly and respectful, albeit tough. Of course, this doesn't always happen: sometimes my combatants view the theories I defend with a mixture of disbelief and bewilderment, even verging on contempt. But usually the wars in this area are profitable and even fun, as people grapple for the truth about whose reality is real. In any case, I persist in philosophizing on these matters in part because I have found that rational arguments can make a substantial difference in people's way of thinking about the world. And given my own commitments, I see it as the best strategy to use in working for a metaphysically more "flexible" world.

II. Feminist Fights with "Social Subordinators"

Another war I fight, which I do not find at all pleasant or rewarding, is with a group that I call "social subordinators," that is, people who are committed to a way of thinking about men and women, males and females, that makes it (normatively) acceptable for women and members of certain ethnic groups to be subordinated to (white) men in various social institutions, and maybe even in political institutions.

These enemies are rarely willing to come out into the open, although sometimes that happens. If he wages war in the public arena, this sort of combatant eschews reason in his methods of intellectual combat, which I believe is intimately connected to the fact that such an opponent does not respect those in the academy whom he is fighting. He relies on invective and ridicule rather than argument; he is animated by certain passions rather than by reason.

Aside from the intellectual combat, such opponents also wage war on the persons of those they take themselves to subordinate rightfully. For example, most women in academia will have stories to tell about sexual harassment, tenure battles, problems publishing, problems with colleagues who belittle them, problems getting respect for their work (particularly for feminist scholarship), and problems with the content of the research being done by colleagues (insofar as it is insidiously antifeminist in its implications).

Battles with these opponents are never enjoyable, in part because such people can never respect those they are fighting against. That lack of respect is linked with rhetorical techniques that one would never use if one were in search of the truth. But then, such opponents are generally interested in subordinating the people with whom they are fighting, not searching for the truth with them. Hence such opponents are ready to sanction any means of "winning" as long as they think it will work.

I should also note that my feminist commitments have been the reason why I have sometimes found myself battling with fellow Christians, whose views of the world — and whose religious beliefs — are challenged by aspects of the feminist position I hold. Such battles are particularly painful because those who fight against the kinds of positions I take not only hate the positions but also tend to demonize me and anyone else who holds them, so that it is almost as if they take themselves to be fighting a religious war. Some Christians take themselves to be licensed to behave in this way toward those whose positions are deeply at odds with their religious beliefs. I find this behavior to be a betrayal of the substantive moral commitments of Christianity, as I will discuss more fully below.

It is worth emphasizing that there are many honorable men and women in the academy working to end the supremacy that certain sorts of groups have traditionally held in this institution and in American intellectual life generally. We would be kidding ourselves, however, if we thought their battle was won, or that a decisive victory was almost in hand. I fully expect to be fighting this battle for as long as I am in academia.

III. Feminist Fights with Feminists

If women are under attack in the academy, one would think they would fight back in a unified manner. But that is not the way things have gone. In some respects this is to be expected. Given how many different kinds of women there are, and how many different kinds of subject matter inform their research, there is no more reason to think there will be a single feminist position than there is to believe there will be a single male position or a single African American position on moral and political matters. So women in the academy disagree. Lamentably, they also attack one another in ways that I find disturbing and regressive for the cause of women. Lamentably, I have been in the midst of this war too, and in some ways this battle is closest to my heart.

Many women look at the history of the academy over the past 150 years and note the extent to which the theorizing done within its walls has played a role in subordinating all sorts of groups, including women, in ways that have supported the entrenched power structure. (Witness the feminist critique of science already mentioned.) Traditionally academic theorizing has been backed up by the researcher's claim to be relying on "reason." But if "reason" is what is used to develop subordinating theories, why should women genuflect to it? Whose reason? Whose authority? they ask.[5] Why not see the appeal to reason as a covert kind of power play on the part of those who use it? Why shouldn't women look for alternative ways of thinking about the world, making use of traditional experiences, emotions, and reactions to life that have been part of the female experience, in ways that challenge the patriarchalist foundation for the authority of their theorizing? Won't such a challenge be a way to fight for justice for women? Isn't it a way of unmasking the pretense of "rightness" that patriarchal theorists persistently maintain (in ways that can be profitably linked with certain postmodernist ways of thinking about the world, about art, and about the academy)?

Much of my research has been directed at answering the last of the questions just enumerated with a "no."[6] But as a result, I have been attacked, sometimes very angrily, by women in the academy who are convinced that my position gives aid and comfort to the enemy. Indeed, many women see the whole field of philosophy — and particularly analytic philosophy — as committed to a way of thinking about the world which is male-biased, and whose theories cannot but be harmful to women. So simply being a "feminist analytic philosopher" is sufficient to attract criticism.

---

5. These sorts of questions are raised by a series of papers in L. Anthony and C. Witt, eds., *A Mind of One's Own* (Boulder, Colo.: Westview Press, 1993).

6. See Jean Hampton, "Feminist Contractarianism," in Anthony and Witt, eds., *A Mind of One's Own.*.

In reply to this criticism, I and other analytic philosophers contend that theorizing in ways that heavily rely on reason is the only way to fight the enemy effectively. In what follows, I want to elaborate on this response.

Consider that for many feminists, the attack on reason is associated with their attack on the traditional idea that there is some kind of intrinsic male and female nature. Feminists have correctly pointed out how little evidence we have about what this nature could be, and how poorly such intrinsic characteristics fit the assumptions of contemporary biology. They also note that this kind of thinking has justified unjust social and political practices. What many of them go on to say is that male and female "natures" are social products, so that any theory of what we are "really" like is necessarily shaped by the society that forms us. These feminists call themselves "pluralists" who believe that there are many points of view, many kinds of "natures" (reflecting diverse societal groupings), and many ways of theorizing about the world, none of which is built into us because of our "nature." All of this is taken to lend support to the idea that there is no universal, culture-independent notion of reason to which we can appeal in constructing any kind of theory, particularly a feminist theory.

However, part of the feminist challenge is to show how society has formed us in ways that are unjust, producing human beings whose development is in some way stunted or deformed because of that injustice, where that stunting or deformity itself has unjust implications — because people wind up either too inclined to want to master others or too inclined to accept mastery. But this means that even "pluralist feminists" have a strong normative commitment to the effect that some points of view (e.g., racist or sexist points of view) are *wrong,* and that some ways of socializing people are unjust or immoral — not just in late-twentieth-century America, but in other times and places as well. Whether or not they explicitly recognize it, these feminists' rejection of unjust forms of socialization and unjust conceptions of human beings is driven by a commitment to objective ideas of human interaction and socialization, which they take it we should endorse, ideals that transcend and have authority over any particular social environment.

The pluralist vision of a better world, in which the oppression of women does not exist, is a vision of women developing in the right — that is, objectively right — way, such that they can flourish and interact with one another in good rather than oppressive or deforming ways. Hence feminists implicitly rely on a moral theory that they take to be the right normative theory for our society and for which they are prepared to fight. For them to claim that it is "just another theory among many" in our society — yet another socially constructed outlook on the world — is to give away the resources they need to defend it as *the right* outlook and the one that should predominate in the construction of our laws and social institutions. A defense for this outlook requires a normative theory — one that can take on and criticize those sexist or racist theories that also exist in our world. To appeal to common beliefs or shared understandings to defend this view is nonsense — the whole problem with our society is that the shared understandings have been, and continue to be, unfavorable to women and minorities. Hence feminists need to be revolutionaries, which means they need to have a theory they can use to challenge the status quo, and which they can defend as better and as right. Their demand is that each of us critically assess our views of the world and one another and reform them in ways that realize the values of justice. But to do this, we must assume that the values of justice trump whatever prejudices we have that are part of our socially created conception of the world, and that these values' authority over us and our social world is something we can recognize by reasoning well.

Indeed, even to say that they are victims of injustice is to invoke a notion that they take to be a challenge to their social world. Feminists who want to fuel reform need not only a way to persuade people of the reality of that injustice, but also a way to defend their prescription for reform. In this task they are philosophizing morally — about injustice, oppression, social justice, and ideal human interaction. To deny this, or to evade this form of reasoning, is to shirk the work they need to do in order to fight effectively and well for their cause.

So feminism needs a moral theory. What moral theory is best? Well, now we have a philosophical question, and an entire tradition of philosophizing about morality and justice is relevant to it. To suppose that women needn't consult such a history is the height of arrogance and a kind of ignorance of the resources that history can provide for those of us struggling to reshape our world in a better way. To deny the importance, power, and relevance of the theorizing of Aristotle, Kant, Hobbes, or Locke to the development of an adequate feminist moral theory is to give up, in my view, on the best chance we have to construct a new and better moral theory that will support the kind of revolution that we want. No philosopher has ever created a theory out of whole cloth; all philosophers have been informed by the thinking of their forebears. We can be so informed, and learn not only from their mistakes but also from their successes. Indeed, feminist rhetoric is informed by the moral terms and ideas crafted by these philosophers (terms such as "rights," "equal dignity," "equal opportunity"). So their ideas can be ours — to use and redeploy, if we are respectful of the wisdom of our intellectual traditions.

Of course, that tradition needs us too. We have ideas to offer that no philosopher has heretofore thought of — ideas that, properly developed, can revolutionize moral philosophizing for the better. But are all the ideas that women are proposing in moral theory today equally good? No. Is the moral theorizing of women immune from criticism? No. What tool do we use to criticize it? Reason. Whose reason? Our reason — that is, the reason that all philosophers from Plato onwards have been committed to affirming.

Let me give you an example of the rational assessment of a feminist moral theory. In 1984 Carol Gilligan published a book called *In a Different Voice*[7] that became a hit. Gilligan argued that women tended to think about morality in a different way than men, and to follow a different developmental path, which she called "The Ethic of Care" in contrast to the male "Ethic of Justice." Many women embraced Gilligan's book, seeing it as developing a woman's moral theory in touch with a deep truth.[8] But other women, myself included, evaluated Gilligan's theory very differently. We challenged Gilligan's evidence for the existence of this voice, arguing not only that her own data were consistent with a variety of other interpretative conclusions, but also that the conclusions she drew about what she heard were only inches away from the traditional view of men as coldly logical and women as warm and fuzzy emotionalists — views associated with all sorts of sexist practices and exclusions (e.g., denying women access to higher education). Indeed, Gilligan's work was actually cited by Sears in the dis-

7. Carol Gilligan, *In a Different Voice* (Cambridge: Harvard University Press, 1984).
8. See Annette Baier, "What Do Women Want in a Moral Theory?" *Nous* 19, no. 1 (March 1985): 53-63.

crimination case of *EEOC v. Sears,* in which Sears was accused of discriminating against women because it had few women in its high-paying sales commission jobs. Sears insisted that women weren't applying for these jobs, and to back up their claim they used an expert witness — a female psychologist — who argued that women weren't applying for these jobs because, as Gilligan has shown, women were interested in *caring,* and hence wanted "caring kinds of jobs" or jobs that allowed them to perform caring tasks (such as mothering). The appellate court bought Sears's argument, and Sears won.

The legal theorist Joan Williams,[9] noting the ease with which Gilligan's ideas were put to use by people who had a stake in maintaining a sexist practice, diagnoses the problem with Gilligan's theory this way: Gilligan, she says, is identifying women with the traditional values of "domesticity," i.e., the values of nurturing, noncompetitive interactions, and pacifism. But this domestic portrait of women is really a Victorian stereotype, which has a dangerous as well as a benign side. It is part of this stereotypical portrait that women are *unable* to compete well in a capitalist society, are less combative and not as tough as men. And, says Williams, Gilligan can't import the "good" side of the stereotype without also importing the bad, as Sears realized to its benefit. Moreover, for those of us females who have trouble, given our crusty, combative personalities, displaying the beneficent nurturing that is characteristic of Gilligan's ethic of care, that ethic is as threatening a portrait of women as anything coming out of the patriarchalists' camp.

Undoubtedly there is something right about Gilligan's celebration of caring, but, as the *Sears* case illustrates, her theory as she advances it is dangerous to the cause of feminism. If we want to keep what is promising about her theory, without importing the bad, we need to use reason to figure out where it goes wrong. And this is in part because advancing a moral theory that inadvertently buys into sexist stereotypes is easy even for women. (Don't we also live in a sexist society? How can we be immune from its effects?) Hence, women's theorizing, like any other theorizing, needs to be scrutinized and evaluated to insure that it does not bear traces of the fruits of injustice. Such assessment requires thought; it is a *rational* assessment. And any woman who cares

9. Joan Williams, "Deconstructing Gender," in *Feminist Jurisprudence,* ed. Patricia Smith (New York: Oxford University Press, 1993), pp. 531-58.

about justice should be eager to submit her moral theory to such rational assessment. If we care about justice, we should not want to introduce ideas that go unchallenged and that inadvertently reinforce the structures of injustice. To use a metallurgical metaphor: members of traditionally excluded groups, if they care about the values of freedom and equality, should not want their moral and political conceptions to escape the fiery seasoning of reason.

IV. How to Fight

As I've indicated, some of the fights I engage in are fun, and some are not. Some of these fights are good for me and my philosophical thinking, and some are relatively useless in bringing about new reflection, new ideas, or new theorizing. Thinking about the fights that are productive as opposed to the fights that aren't is a good starting point for considering which sorts of culture wars are good for the academy, and which are bad.

The first thing to reflect upon if you are engaged in a battle is how to fight effectively for your cause. And if there is one thing that my experience has convinced me of, it is that you don't fight effectively if you fight in a way that is disrespectful, disparaging, hateful, spiteful, mean-minded, or emotional. Ironically, these are very common methods of attack. I suspect that for many people who are angry at those whom they fight, some form of what I will call a "belittling" strategy is emotionally satisfying and at least *seems* effective given that, if it is done well, it seems to put the opponents' views "in their place" — that is, a *low* place. But in the end it isn't really effective, because such a strategy never really convinces the opponents. In fact, it usually makes them confirmed enemies, even more hostile to your views than they were before you started. This is, I believe, in part because of the legacy of disrespect: to relate to someone in a way that fails to take that person seriously as a person is to invoke his or her anger. Even if your doing so is in the service of what you take to be a good cause, this way of relating isn't worth it because, whatever short-term rhetorical advantage you might gain from it, in the long term it makes those who have witnessed or received your rhetoric *less* likely to believe you, not more likely.

Another reason belittling forms of argument fail is that they virtually never take seriously the substance of the positions they attack. Almost all positions in academia, particularly the ones that are well entrenched, have some substantive basis. People believe them for *reasons* — sometimes not very good reasons, but reasons nonetheless. Unless those reasons are uncovered and directly addressed, they continue to exercise their sway over the minds of those who are susceptible to them. Hence a strategy that fails to take on those reasons and defeat them is going to leave untouched the basis for the support of the opponents' position. Belittling strategies mock, disparage, laugh at, ridicule, and demonize, but they do not undermine the rational basis for the position's support. Hence whatever short-term rhetorical value they may have, they do little to break the hold of that position on the minds of those attracted to it.

The fact that belittling strategies are immoral as well as ineffective is important for another reason, having to do with the way respecting even your enemies is a fundamental precept of the Christian faith. If part of the reason you engage in a war of ideas has to do with your concern for justice, which involves among other things working for a world in which all persons are accorded dignity and respect, then your commitment to these values necessitates that you adhere to them when you fight. If you do not, you are hypocritically commending to others values that you yourself are prepared to put aside when you believe it is in your interest to do so. This is a betrayal of those values. I also take it to be a betrayal of Christianity insofar as Christianity involves, above all else, the endorsement of the idea that we are all equal and valuable in the eyes of the Lord. These values do not mean that you can't fight hard, or tough, or put lots of pressure on your opponent. Treating people with respect is importantly different from (and in certain ways opposed to) being "nice" to them.

Finally, I believe you have to fight your wars in a way that involves rational reflection. I am, as I have explained, deeply committed to reason and rational reflection insofar as it engages the best part of human beings, not the worst. I see certain feminist criticisms of theorizing in science, philosophy, and social science not as attacks on reason, but as attacks on theorizing that uses bad reasoning and poor argumentation full of bias or prejudice or emotional appeals. As John Stuart Mill complained with respect to the opponents of woman suffrage and women's equality in his day, their positions were almost never defended, and they were never defended *well* using the standard tools of reason.[10] So, for example, biologists who paint a picture of women or members of certain ethnic groups as inferior invariably do experimentation or extrapolate from data in ways that violate the normative methodological standards of science.

From Socrates to the present day, the project of philosophy is based on the idea that to the extent that you can get people to think, you loosen the grip of ideology on their minds; help them escape from the blinding effects of emotion, prejudice, and unjust social custom; and enable them to recognize rhetorical trickery designed to obscure the truth. Yet to face an opponent committed to reason also requires a kind of faith, a faith that I think may be tremendously difficult for all of us — particularly those of us who feel strongly about a certain point of view. To reason with others, you have to listen to them. Not just listen to them, but *hear* them, take them seriously, consider the extent to which they are saying something that might be right. To take such an attitude toward someone whose views are anathema to you is extremely hard. Indeed, some might worry that taking such an attitude is in and of itself a betrayal to the cause for which you are fighting. How can you take seriously, for example, disreputable sexist or racist views, political theories that you believe will foment injustice, or theoretical portrayals of human beings that are inconsistent with your idea of their worth or value? But taking even bad views seriously isn't a betrayal of your own values — for two reasons. First, if you are right, then taking your opponent seriously shouldn't frighten you, because there is nothing that your opponent can say that would show you to be wrong. If you are frightened to take him seriously, then you're scared, and your fear is a manifestation of a lack of faith. So *not* taking him seriously is the real faithless act. Second, your inability to take him seriously is a betrayal of your commitment to the truth; for if he is right, then if you care about the truth you should care about listening to him. In my view, there is no way that any person could be right who would deny the equal dignity of all human beings. So even if someone who chal-

10. See John Stuart Mill, "The Subjection of Women," in *Essays on Sex Equality* by John Stuart Mill and Harriet Taylor, ed. Alice Rossi (Chicago: University of Chicago Press, 1970), p. 126.

lenges this idea is saying things deeply offensive, you should not be fearful of listening to him, challenging his ideas, or engaging him about the defensibility of the foundations of his ideas, because you should have confidence in the view that he is wrong. You shouldn't *need* to belittle him.

There is another problem with those who would fight without reason. To the extent that they persuade, they persuade without rational foundation. Their converts have the idea that they want, but it exists ungrounded and hence is capable of being shifted, changed, perverted. They are, in other words, ripe for counter-conversion. One of the problems I see with undergraduates today is that they are so little able to reflect upon the messages they get both in the classroom and in the media that their opinions are often as changeable as the weather, as unfixed as sand, as manipulable as putty. An effective strategy should strive for a solidity of thinking and commitment that will stand our students and ourselves in good stead no matter what opposing forces they, or we, may meet.

Perhaps most of all, those who fight using the tools of reason are committed to *respecting* their opponents. To appeal to others' reason in an argument is a way of saying to them that you understand that they will make a choice about whether or not to agree with you; hence it eschews the idea of rhetorically coercing them to take your side. A person who is committed to rationally reflecting with her opponent is rejecting the strategy of trying to control a person's thinking so as to insure that he arrives at the "right" conclusion. And thus she is respecting him — not as a virtuous person, or a smart person, or a person who satisfies any social ideal (although he could also be any of these things), but as a person who can and ought to choose how to lead his own life and how to think about the world as he does so. Such respect can lead to friendship, and friendship can enable both parties to think more flexibly, openly, and profitably about the other's position.

Given that modern constitutional democracies are still not societies in which there is widespread agreement that all people should be given the same rights and opportunities, we have an obligation as thinkers to be committed to arguing with, and thus respecting, our fellow human beings to persuade opponents of that idea and thus to change their minds.

"But they won't change their minds, so we have to use whatever tools we can so that our side (which is the right side) will win," some might say. But that I take to be the counsel of hate, a counsel that is not only morally disreputable but also ineffective. Giving up on someone is a way of hating that person, and while there may be some who merit this response, they are highly unusual. Most of our opponents are human beings who, like ourselves, are mixtures of good and bad, and who, despite the bad, deserve the same respect that we believe we should be accorded. To give way to this counsel of hate is also deeply violative of the spirit of Christian love and Christian values. That it is ineffective is, I think, intrinsically connected to the fact that it is violative of those values, because by violating those values, this hateful strategy will make the position that is being commended less rather than more likely to be accepted by those who are the recipients of that hate.

In the end, I would argue that anyone who shares Socrates' delight in searching for wisdom with her fellow human beings should not want to give up that pursuit and should be committed to engaging in the search for wisdom in ways that not only attempt to realize, but also to manifest, the equal dignity and value of all human beings.

PART THREE

Postmodernism and the Standing of Religious Belief

WAYNE C. BOOTH

Deconstruction as a Religious Revival

I. The Problem of Definition

Few terms in our language, pre- or postmodernist, are as ambiguous and as full of rival definitions as "deconstruction" and "religion," though "modernist" and "postmodernist" would be close rivals. And few claims about such terms could produce more contradictory responses than the one I want to explore here — namely, that the most important of the moves by deconstructionists have so closely resembled the best of traditional religious inquiry as to deserve the label "religious."

Many who are deeply committed to religion have seen the deconstructionists as enemies. Some deconstructionists have claimed overt and implacable antipathy to anything called religious belief or commitment. Yet anyone who has read much serious theology and who then reads closely and widely in the astonishingly diverse works labeled deconstructionist will be struck by how often the mind is plunged into the same troubled waters, hoping, often in great confusion, for some escape to firmer ground. Even without such hard labor through threatening hours, a quick glance at recent bibliographies will show that innumerable "deconstructionists" have seen themselves as deliberately engaged in religious inquiry, and that many a scholar trained in traditional theologies has been treating deconstructionists, even those who call themselves unbelievers, as potential allies.[1]

Thus in one sense my topic, though surprising to some, will seem to others banal. Deconstructionists like Geoffrey Hartman, Hillis Miller, and Mark Taylor will rightly want to ask, "So what is new?" Yet I have been strongly criticized by some academic friends who think deconstruction is destroying their values: "Your topic is absurd." Others are now claiming — and hoping — that "deconstruction is dead"; that it was a "flash in the pan."[2] Such disparity dramatizes a central question that every ecumenical project like this one should face honestly: Why attempt to uncover the common ground that supports those who think they inhabit different worlds — especially when many of them claim there is no such thing as "ground" at all, let alone ground that is shared? I return to that question briefly toward the end.

To suggest, however haltingly, that many deconstructionists' moves not only aid and abet religious inquiry but are in themselves religious, even when the movers claim to be atheists — that is itself a "move" that obviously requires some difficult definition, definition of a kind that some would want to call "deconstruction." What is more, the very notion of "definition" meets curious obstacles here, since many of the thinkers we're talking about reject any possibility of clear definition,[3] while others will claim that without absolutely clear, consensual definition, no real inquiry

1. The items listed in my bibliography amount to a crude selection — no doubt already outdated — from an avalanche of such studies.

2. These are usually critics who have read little deconstruction, and who lump scores of authors under a single label. Their ignorance of our scene, traveling under the banner of "true scholarship," is the counterpart of the blank indifference of many traditional religionists. After giving a version of this article as a talk at the Calvin College conference "Christianity and Culture in the Crossfire," I was crushed to find that at least three professors of religion in my audience (not from Calvin College) had never even heard of Derrida and really had no clue about what I'd been trying to say. "Who is this man, Derridoff?" one of them asked me at breakfast the following morning. What could better dramatize the unfortunate divorce of "frontline" theorizing from the interests of the general "religious" public?

3. I was chatting with a well-known deconstructionist recently and praised the popular manual of style by my colleague Joseph Williams: *Style: Toward Clarity and Grace* (Chicago: University of Chicago Press, 1990). My companion burst into mocking laughter and explained that anyone who makes clarity a standard of good English is benighted.

can be pursued. My claim is that regardless of our definitions, religious thought can no longer utterly reject either postmodernism in general — the new movements of the last forty years — or the primary moves of those postmodernists who have either called themselves deconstructionists or had the label applied by others. Whether deconstructionism is now fading or will soon fade into being seen as just one major moment in twentieth-century history, it must be viewed as a fundamentally important moment in the history of religion. The best deconstructionists should be seen, by those who care for religious inquiry, not as the satanic destroyers that too many humanists and religious thinkers have portrayed them as, but rather as members of a kind of coast-guard crew who have carried out a mission to rescue a pathetic figure, Genuinely Religious Rhetoric, that had been shouting, "Help! I'm drowning in the cold waters of scientism."[4] As for that "opposite camp," the postmodernists who profess atheism, I have a half-secret, feeble hope that in thinking about these issues they will be led to acknowledge the deeper implications of what they are up to.

It is important at the beginning to underline the double nature of my claim: it is not just that deconstruction has rendered *talk about* religious questions respectable; it has restored *religious inquiry* to respectable status in many academic fields. Serious religious questions have been dragged out of what had become one small corner of divinity schools and have now intruded, at various paces (the pace depending in part on the quality of the mobilized opposition), into departments of literature, history, sociology, political science, philosophy, and law. Indeed, the effects can also be found, though perhaps less dramatically, in the natural sciences.[5]

---

4. This is not the place to record the history of religious decline in the academy. We all know about the "secularization" of all *genuine* scholarly inquiry, as traced in other essays here.

5. It is hard to know, of course, whether deconstructionist underminings of positivist scientific language have contributed much to the recent outburst of cosmological and cosmogonic inquiry among physicists. Obviously scientists who have really thought hard about the mystifying paradoxes produced by quantum physics and astrophysics did not need deconstruction to teach them that beneath our fixities lurk threatening ambiguities, "unintelligibilities," and even certain kinds of "abyss." But the fact is that an astonishing amount of "scientific" literature now appears under titles like *The Conscious Universe* or *The Mind of God,* some of it with elaborate references

An essential task throughout will be to grapple with that forever slippery term, "religion." It is hard to think of any term more polymorphous, even perverse. I have several friends who, in the half-definition I'm coming to, qualify as deeply religious yet who themselves claim to be enemies of, or at least indifferent to, what *they* call religion. On the other hand, we all know fanatics of this or that official religion who claim that all other so-called religions don't really deserve the name. Some of these self-proclaimed religionists, but by no means all, do not in my definition of religion deserve the term "religious"; we need some other label for them — perhaps *gee*-ligion, with an exclamation point, or *de*-ligion or *dis*-ligion, because they wipe out most of what to me are essentials. Some of these, the ones that offer little more than a self-praising cheering up before Sunday brunch, we might call *me*-ligions. In any case, no matter what definitions we land on, we ourselves will be committing evaluations: if our definition is accepted, that means we have given a badge of approval to the accepter. If our definition is rejected, it will be because the rejector is sure that it was chosen in order to eliminate his or her absolutely religious religion.

The three standard ways of dealing with this near chaos are, first, avoid definition entirely, since "religion" is nothing more than a catchall term — what I've even heard called a garbage bag. Richard Rorty recently claimed that whenever religion enters the discussion, any sensible person will just withdraw, and conversation stops.[6] Second, one can proclaim the one true definition that best fits one's preferred denomination — or denominations. Finally, one can attempt, as William James did in his wonderful *Varieties of Religious Experience,* a definition that might in some way cover the common ground underlying all or most religions. Obviously whether or how one uses the label "religion" in referring to any or all of the movements called deconstruction or post-structuralism will depend on which of these we choose.

---

to current "deconstructions." See, e.g., Menas Kafatos and Robert Nadeau, *The Conscious Universe: Part and Whole in Modern Physical Theory* (New York: Springer-Verlag, 1990), or call up "God and Science" on your library's computer. Ten years ago the flood of such work was already impressive; see my attempt to view scientific cosmologists as disguised theologians: "Systematic Wonder: The Rhetoric of Secular Religions," *Journal of the American Academy of Religion* 53, no. 3 (1985): 677-702.

6. See Richard Rorty, "Religion as Conversation Stopper," *Common Knowledge* (spring 1994): 1-6.

In current terms the difference between options two and three, the particularist and the ecumenical, is sometimes called the Yale/Chicago split.[7] Labels like that are of course reductive, even unfair, since they polarize extremes that few on either side would embrace. Professor Lindbeck and others at Yale and Professor Tracy and others at Chicago cannot be fit into neatly contrasting categories. I am of course tempted to use these aggressive labels because that would place my own university on the ecumenical side I favor, leaving the Yalies abused and annoyed. But I'll resist that and simply call the two camps by the totally objective terms "dogmatists" and "pluralists." No, strike that! Let's deal instead with "particularists" and "common-groundists."

On the one hand are those who believe you have not in any real sense defined a religion as genuine until you have described it in its full particularity, including the precise details of its unique foundation story and its unique rituals. A genuinely religious believer, under this definition, is one who is certain of the unique validity of his or her particular foundation story and most or all of the details of doctrine which that story is claimed to embody. Religious inquiry for such a believer consists mainly in the pursuit of what that uniquely true story has to say about our origins and how we should live our lives. Any comparisons with other religions must be equally particularist: you can tolerate them, even respect them, but you cannot fit them under any umbrella that covers you. The best they deserve is something like "misguided religions" or "partial religions." In other words, religion for them is not to be found in any ecumenical or pluralistic definition of *common* characteristics but in the full, thick, intratextual description of the details of one faith, one ritual, one communal practice, and one scriptural embeddedness of individual denominations.

The opposite approach digs down to the common ground that such particular religions share. Though common-groundists may in the long run make judgments of relative worth, what is at their center is what is shared, not what makes them peculiar. And if they make value judgments against some professions of religion, as I have already revealed that I do, they are still likely to leave not a single one clearly at

7. Scott Holland, "How Do Stories Save Us? Two Contemporary Theological Responses," *Conrad Grebel Review* 12 (spring 1994): 131-53.

the top of the hierarchy but rather a plurality of the "great religions," contrasted with the not-so-great or utterly defective.

The search for common ground is not easy, and it always makes me think of an experience of Professor David Tracy, Catholic theologian, as he met for several years with leaders of other "great religions" seeking to formulate what they shared. Meeting annually with Buddhists, Muslims, Jews, Catholics, and Hindus, as I remember his account, Tracy would return looking discouraged. "We found little or nothing this year." But one year not long ago he came back much buoyed up, obviously feeling that the meetings had at last proved successful. When asked what they had agreed on, he said, "We all agreed that something went radically wrong with creation."[8]

No matter how we feel about the search for common ground, our choice between the particularist and the common-groundist definitional routes will determine how we treat deconstructionists and other postmodernists. If we follow James and pursue the common ground, as I shall do below, our task will be to discover not whether all deconstructionists or post-modernists, lumped together, have somehow contributed to religious inquiry; obviously many have not. Rather, we ask whether any one of them exhibits, when probed to the core, the common elements we claim are shared by all genuine religions. Obviously as we do such probing of any one faith, we must attempt the "thick" description advocated by the particularists, asking whether that faith shares *fully* the common ground we have found in the others. But from the perspective of particularists, our generalized quest will still always look "thin," since we finally put what are to us superficial differences to one side and stress the common core.

The particularist/common-ground distinction automatically divides our inquiry into two parts. First, addressing mainly the *particularists,* I shall claim that regardless of how strongly they object to this or that doctrine of any postmodernist, the whole flood of postmodernisms, and especially of deconstructionisms, has performed a religious service. Then, addressing mainly the *common-groundists,* I shall argue that one particular deconstructionist, Jacques Derrida, shares their common ground — or at least enough of it to justify inviting him into the church porch.

8. I can be quite sure that Tracy would by now report this experience rather differently. After all, he himself did not witness his own face on his return from the two different experiences.

II. Postmodernism as a Resurrection
of Humane Rhetoric

If one is a particularist, if one has a fully developed religion and claims to know that only such a fully developed religion deserves the name "religion" at all, can it make any sense to claim that the "crossfires" of postmodernism have yielded a religious revival? It's true that many individual deconstructionists have openly declared their commitment to this or that traditional religion, employing religious terms of traditional kinds, Jewish or Christian; it is also true that some other postmodern positions have been embraced by communicants in various religions.[9] For such folks, my claims here will not seem utterly wild, since they have themselves experienced no irreconcilable conflict.

But the fact remains that most postmodernists have said a sharp "no" to questions like, "Do my claims constitute a religion?" or "Does my inquiry support the inquiry of those others who are openly religious?" Indeed, it's not hard to find deconstructionists who, despite their claim to undermine all direct, simple assertion, declare themselves unequivocally, essentialistically atheistic.[10]

In short, most committed particularists will be rightly suspicious of my project. For them, you don't have a religion until you have a full panoply of ritual, commandments, beliefs, and behaviors, what some particularists call a "cultural-linguistic model" or "grammar." "You just don't have a real religion," they say, "until you have something resembling mine in all its fullness." From this perspective only a very small number of postmodernist positions could be called religious, and most, perhaps even all of them, appear to be dismissible finally as untrue, if not actually dangerous.

How then can I claim that even for the true believer who considers the various postmodernist ploys a disastrous undermining of true religion, deconstructionists along with other postmodernists have been

9. I know a Mormon professor of philosophy, James E. Faulconer, who has found a deep harmony between Mormon theology and some versions of post-Heideggerian claims.

10. It's easier to find openly professed atheism among those scientists and scholars who cling to the grand debunking project of the Enlightenment as traced by Nicholas Wolterstorff in this volume. Richard Rorty, in the article cited above, claiming to maintain the Enlightenment norms, calls himself an atheist or atheistic many times.

producing a revival of religious inquiry in fields that formerly professed utter indifference to religious questions?

The answer lies in the relation of different notions of what constitutes a respectable rhetoric to different notions of what religion is. As I've argued at length elsewhere, the intellectual respectability of religion has always depended on the respectability of forms of rhetoric that were discredited in what Wolterstorff calls elsewhere in this book the "Grand Project," the search for scientific certainties.[11] My basic claim here is that the almost equally grand project of some postmodernists has been to discredit the discrediting: not just to show that the very language used by the discreditors did not deserve the credit it had been granted, but that it had ruled out questions that deserve to be restored to full intellectual respectability.

First, the vast, amorphous movement at its best has shown that the rhetoric of positivism was radically disingenuous and incoherent; it had within itself the seeds of its own destruction. By revealing the ideological underpinnings of even the most objectivist inquiries, deconstructionism and its allies have forced all inquirers into territory previously thought to be reserved for theologians. Every academic discipline, including the hard sciences, has been nudged to admit that when probed rigorously its foundations look much like the foundations of what was traditionally called religion: they cannot be established with hard proofs; they can only be discussed in the *kind* of language, or rhetoric, always employed by theologians.[12]

Second, by throwing into question all of the Grand Project's disproofs of religion, the movement has resurrected, as it were, the lord God and all of her angels: God is no longer dead but perhaps has been alive and well all the while. Indeed, every disproof of religious rhetoric from the early Enlightenment on through modernism is now forced into reconsideration, and serious religious inquiry has been invited back into the academic parlor.

11. Wayne Booth, "Rhetoric and Religion: Are They Essentially Wedded?" in *Radical Pluralism and Truth,* ed. Werner G. Jeanrond and Jennifer L. Rike (New York: Crossroad, 1991), pp. 62-80.

12. Some claim that the undermining of certainties has been produced strictly within the Grand Project itself, with such events as Gödel's proof that no mathematical system can demonstrate its own first principles, or the developments in quantum theory out of the uncertainty principle of Heisenberg. Others have clearly been influenced by critical work from the "humanists" and "antihumanists."

A full pursuit of this double claim would require a book in itself, but it might be summarized like this: deconstructionism and its buddies have liberated the academic world to reconsider every question about metaphysics, ontology, cosmology, and cosmogony that the positivistic hardheads thought they had settled. Even the new works that have avoided words like *god, religion, morality,* and *ethics* have constituted a vast invasion by essentially religious questions into fields that had mistakenly believed they had ruled them out.[13] Thus the world has been liberated, or indeed forced, to engage again in theology; the widespread joke of thirty years ago — namely, that theology was the only academic subject without a subject matter — was suddenly rendered pointless. Or we could say that "the book," the collection of narratives of our relation to God, of what might be called "rhetorical proofs," was discarded by the Grand Project, and that book — a collection of actual books, of course — is back at the center. For the first time in modern history, the presumably reliable language of Enlightenment disproofs of religion has been systematically thrown into question. The very language that had been used by language philosophers earlier in the century to discard not just religion but metaphysics and epistemology and genuine moral argument, is now seen as just another form of questionable metaphysics.

If I'm right, then, the very moves that have worried some traditional believers, whether in traditional religions or traditional humanisms, might well have cheered them up. We have been blessed by a reminder of what many theologians had taught but that modernism had forgotten: not just how ambiguous and un-pin-downable are terms like *religious, god, atheism, essence, substance,* and *disproof,* but how everything we say depends on our theology.

Thus, despite the excesses of some prophets of what Paul Ricoeur calls "the rhetoric of suspicion," these past three decades have produced an opening out to the renovation of old religious syntheses and the exploration of new ones. In short, once we look beneath surfaces that

13. Kenneth Burke's *The Rhetoric of Religion: Studies in Logology* (Boston: Beacon Press, 1961) had already performed this move of restoring religious inquiry through a restoration of rhetorical thought. But relatively few people attended to his revolutionary work — and besides, he himself could not embrace the full religious implications of his own rediscovery of the ontological argument for the existence of God.

often do seem quite silly and too often are carelessly written, we find that the jumble of overlapping movements has been performing a noble work, often unwittingly: by throwing into question all *ir*religious inquiry, these troublesome folk have been flooding the previously arid academic world with fertile religious inquiry.

All of this claim ultimately depends, however, on the "common-groundist" definition that I come to now, as I deal more explicitly with one branch of the movements I have been lumping together as post-modernism.

III. A Further Effort at Definition, with Five Marks of All Religions

To celebrate, as I'm doing, the achievement of the rhetorical revolution, as produced by widely diverse postmodernists with their disproofs of disproof, is not the same as showing why any one of the new languages or new ploys is in itself in any sense really religious. All I have shown so far is that they have restored legitimacy to questions long discredited by most academics. What can we say then about the charge made by many particularist believers that those three decades have been flooded not with new invitations to religion but with new invitations to blank nihilism? In discrediting various positivist moves, have they not also shattered the foundations of all serious inquiry?

That question cannot be answered by lumping together all post-modernists. Paradoxically, it requires combining a search for common ground, a general definition of religion, with a highly particularist look at one or another of the postmodernists, to see if he or she shares that common ground. And to perform that close look honestly, we should choose a thinker who claims not to be religious and who has alarmed a great many particularists. Surely the best case will be Jacques Derrida.

Thus I am forced, belatedly here, to grapple with the age-old ecumenical problem: how to define what constitutes *the* core shared by all genuine religions. After fumbling with that hard one, I shall ask whether Derrida belongs within that core.

A century ago, William James, pursuing this search for a common-ground definition, explained why such a search for an umbrella will always dissatisfy true believers of the particularist kind. Like him I can predict angry responses: "Call *that* a religion? Nonsense. That's actually a clever disguise invented by the devil." But James's route, though not his precise definition, can perhaps help us bypass at least some of the pointless and profitless quarreling that fills our culture.

James's actual definition doesn't quite do the full job needed in looking at deconstructionists like Derrida. Concentrating as it does on the deep emotional feelings that he saw as common to all religious persons, it would rule out the writing of most deconstructionists, because they have not talked much about such matters as spiritual exaltation or the bliss of prayer. His definition seems to me more a definition of religious psychology, the *feelings* of the believer — a definition of a kind of person rather than a religion. Here it is:

> Religion, therefore, as I now ask you arbitrarily to take it, shall mean for us the feelings, acts, and experiences of individual men in their solitude, so far as they apprehend themselves to stand in relation to whatever they may consider the divine.[14]

It is surely understandable that James, a philosophical psychologist, would settle on the psychology of religious experience, the feelings of men and women in their solitude. And he was certainly right to insist on that one strong element: a deep emotional commitment felt as somehow connected with something larger than and in some sense independent of the individual: what he rightly calls the divine. But I want for now to include under the religious umbrella more than those persons who express ecstatic feelings of connectedness to this or that god. We need to broaden it even further and include those whose *feelings* of connection may seem relatively bland but who do claim not just that their feelings, but also their moral choices, are connected to, or in some sense dependent on, a *whole* that they do not themselves create: a *cosmos,* if you will, that yields not just feelings of connectedness *in one's solitude* but commandments for certain behaviors, along with implicit reasons for why one should obey the commands.[15] Obviously for my purposes

14. William James, *The Varieties of Religious Experience* (Cambridge: Harvard University Press, 1985; first published, 1902), p. 34.

15. Such definitions were fairly common until quite recently. William Ernest Hocking defined religion as "a passion for righteousness, and for the spread of righ-

here, such definitions, broad as they are, need a bit of further broadening. At the same time, our quest will be trivialized if we broaden our definition to include *all* commitments, *all* "world views," as M. Scott Peck did in his best-selling, late-seventies *The Road Less Traveled.* "Since everyone has some understanding — some world view, no matter how limited or primitive or inaccurate — everyone has a religion. This fact, not widely recognized, is of the utmost importance: everyone has a religion."[16]

In place of a flat propositional definition, then, I suggest five marks that I think are found in all who believe in, and practice, some sort of religion. My list is sure to leave out some "essential" that you care about. (Remember, however, that as you add more marks, you move closer and closer to the particularists.) For this project it is more important not to multiply excluding marks than to overlook marks that any one group would consider essential.

One: Insistence that the world is somewhat flawed.

Two: Insistence that the flaws be seen in the light of the Unflawed.

These two marks, intertwined, are best revealed by the David Tracy anecdote: "Something went wrong with creation." His report of the

---

teousness, conceived as a cosmic demand," in *Living Religions and a World Faith* (New York: Macmillan, 1940). Matthew Arnold's oft-quoted definition claimed that one is religious if he or she has a strong commitment to the authority of the moral law, believing in the reality of a "power not ourselves that makes for righteousness." John Updike gives a more up-to-date version in his memoirs: "I would define religion," he says, not "only in the form of the world's barbaric and even atrocious religious orthodoxies but in the form of any private system, be it adoration of Elvis Presley or hatred of nuclear weapons, . . . that submerges in a transcendent concern the grimly finite facts of our individual human case. . . . [R]eligion . . . is our persistence, against all the powerful . . . evidence that we are insignificant accidents within a vast uncaused churning, in feeling that our life is a story, with a pattern and a moral and an inevitability. . . ." John Updike, *Self-Consciousness: Memories* (New York: Fawcett Press, 1990), p. 239. His whole chapter, "On Being a Self Forever," is a challenging account of his effort to decide in just what sense he is himself "religious."

16. M. Scott Peck, *The Road Less Traveled: A New Psychology of Love, Traditional Values, and Spiritual Growth* (New York: Simon and Schuster, 1974), pp. 185ff. It is obviously true that everyone cares more about some things than some other things, and in doing so everyone has at least a truncated "worldview": some things are more important in the "world" than others. But to call all such commitments "religions" makes the term meaningless, just as to insist on a particularist definition rules out dialogue.

discovery was not just that "something *is* wrong with the world" or that "there's a lot of stuff in the world that I personally disapprove of or grieve over." Everybody believes that: not just devout Muslims and Catholics and Calvinists but also *me*-ligionists and atheists and drug addicts and serial killers all think something could and should be better about the world — even if it is only that "I ought to have more drugs available" or "I don't have enough corpses yet buried in my cellar" or "Why can't I get every day the feelings I get in that new entertainment church on Sunday morning?"

No: to qualify as a religion, a belief system must relate the first mark to the second one: it must imply a story, a master narrative that says, "Something *went wrong* with *creation.*" It's not just "I don't like some things about it," but rather, "Some things are wrong when judged by what would be right, by what a full rightness would demand, by what the whole of creation as I see it implies as the way things should be but are not." In other words, there was, and in some sense still is, a fall, a brokenness, a decline from what would have been better to what is in fact at best a combination of the better — some ideal — and the worse. Some Buddhists, I gather, would reverse this temporal scheme: not a "fall" but a "rise." But to do that does not destroy the real meaning of "something went wrong": it either was or could have been better.

Religious believers in this sense will include all who experience a kind of double vision: a vision of a possible past or present or future order or cosmos superior to the way things actually work now, entailing an awareness that much of what we experience seems out of whack in that order: *the times are out of joint, dis*-ordered. The cosmos has moved toward chaos; the second law of thermodynamics is threatening not just physically but morally. The origins have gone askew, developing a vast collection of flaws. It is not just — to repeat — that I'd *like* it to be different, for personal reasons. It *ought* to be different, because there are real reasons for seeing it as broken. I have at least a dim notion of what it might mean to be fixed, and I know that what's wrong about it is *wrong,* not just unpleasant.

The first half of this mark-pair, the awareness of awfulness, is, as I said, shared by most people. I suspect that more of us these days are talking about things going downhill than at any time since World War II or the Cuban missile crisis. Nobody needs particular crises like the spectacularly bad weather blows of this year or the Bosnian troubles to sense that if things can go wrong, they will — that, as the popular vulgar license plate puts it, shit happens. But this first mark does not qualify as religious unless it is linked with the second, when someone realizes not just that shit happens but that it has always happened, from the beginning or almost from the beginning — and that "shit" is defined by an elusive notion of its opposite, an order or cosmos which in some sense judges the happening as wrong.

Three, emerging from the first two: All whom I'm calling genuinely religious will somehow see themselves as in some inescapable sense a part of the brokenness. It's not just other people — those terrorists out there, say — who are out of joint. *I* am. I'm not as good or kind or effective or smart as I ought to be. Even the best of us, even the strongest, the purest, the humblest, are inherently lacking, deficient, in need of further repair, or, if you prefer the words, we are sinful or guilty. I am an inseparable part of a cosmos that produced this flawed fraction of itself, including in that fraction a sense of regret about the flaws.

Four, following inescapably from the first three: The cosmos I believe in, the cosmos I feel gratitude toward for its gift of my very existence and its implied ideals, the cosmos that is in its manifestations in my world in some degree broken — my cosmos calls upon me to do something about the brokenness, to do what I can in the repair job, working to heal both my own deficiencies and to aid my fellow creatures in healing theirs.

Five, a corollary of the other four: Whenever my notion of what the cosmos requires of me conflicts with my immediate wishes or impulses, I ought to surrender to its commandments, rather than pursuing what is easiest or most pleasant or most reassuring to my present sensations or wishes: what Wolterstorff in his essay calls my everyday programming. Our impulses, our immediate wishes, *ought* to be overridden whenever they conflict with responsibility to cosmic commandments. We have *obligations* not just to others but to the Other.

Most readers who profess one or another of the official religions will have noticed that I've not mentioned a sixth mark, one that many traditional religions would place as number one and that is missing from most prominent postmodern accounts. Most major traditional religions have seen their foundational cosmos as not so tightly organized as to prevent divine interventions in the order of things: this or that powerful god or gods is both able and willing to modify the original creation providentially, or even, as one reading of the story of Job has it, capriciously. The ultimate cosmic powers have thus in most official religions usually been powerful manipulators of our lives — sometimes actually increasing the brokenness, as seen from our limited point of view, but usually promising (as in the Judeo-Christian-Muslim traditions) a healing of the brokenness, either with temporary miracle now or with some final granting of paradise to the few who deserve it.

T. S. Eliot puts this promise most beautifully at the end of his *Four Quartets*. After many wonderful portrayals of the brokenness, the destructive fires of life as we live it, and many glimpses of the divine, symbolized by the rose in the garden, he concludes:

> And all will be well and
> All manner of thing will be well
> When the tongues of flames are in-folded
> Into the crowned knot of fire
> When the rose and the fire are one.[17]

In religions that add this mark of a providential lord attending to petitions, or that start with it, while it remains true that we must do what we can to heal ourselves or the world, our final hope rests only on what God or Allah or Yahweh has in mind, or has had in mind from the beginning, and on how close we can come to harmony with his or her will and power.

This mark, crucial to many particularists, would rule out of religion many that my common-groundist project wants to rule in. The miracle mark is not found in most deconstructionists. Indeed, many devout believers even within the Christian-Judaic tradition have condemned this mark as reducing our responsibilities to a kind of cheap bargaining or bribery: our reason for obedience to our cosmos becomes, many have lamented, merely an attempt to get paid back at the end.[18] It seems clear that if I were to make this mark essential here I would simply wipe out not only most of the actual deconstructionist moves, including

17. T. S. Eliot, *Collected Poems: 1909-1962* (London: Faber and Faber, 1963), p. 223.

18. For a splendid history of religious and secular "bribery," one that wrestles with the moral paradoxes implicit in the story of Christ's redemption, or "buy-back," of mankind's sins, see John T. Noonan Jr., *Bribes: The Intellectual History of a Moral Idea* (Berkeley: University of California Press, 1984).

Derrida's; most of this essay would have to be scrapped. I would be reduced to the claim I made in part two, that the postmodernists' rhetoric has at some points provided a genuine (though not in itself necessarily religious) reopening in which all those who think of themselves as irreligious will have to consider religious questions once again.

IV. Religious Concepts in Derrida's Version of Deconstruction

I am suggesting that any intellectual position that can be shown to exhibit the five marks is a religion, regardless of what it calls itself. And as every reader will expect by now, I am claiming that Derrida exhibits all five marks.

From one perspective on *some* readings of *some* versions of deconstructionism, my pursuit here would be considered just plain absurd. It would indeed be absurd if I tried to show that every version of deconstructionism exhibits all or most of the first five marks. It would be easy if I chose one or another deconstructionist who openly embraces this or that particular religion. But obviously our question carries real bite only when applied to someone like Derrida who claims to be essentially un-pin-downable, essentially anti-essentialist, implacably against any claim that he is worshiping any kind of divinity.

To prove that the master of all who *don't* know is doing theology would take maybe a lifetime, and even when after decades my proof was completed and the great slider was pinned down, he would immediately set out to prove that I was wrong. Nevertheless, his work reveals to anyone who reads it closely that he has always been wandering in religious territory and that in recent years he's been on the move, sliding closer and closer to a final move that I can only predict — or at least hope for: an open confession of some sort of religious commitment.

How does he look when considered in the light of the five marks? *Marks one and two: the brokenness as genuinely broken.* Can there be any question that Derrida sees us as living in a world radically deficient as compared not just with what we could wish it to be but with what it *ought* to be? Derrida has exposed us as living in a twenty-five-hundred-year-old dream, the Grand Project, the dream of a world that can be fully understood, a reliable, reasonable world, a world in which full understanding is finally available to us, at least in principle. For him we actually live in a world of perpetual elusiveness; every statement about it can be shown, as earlier negative theologians insisted, to be disappointingly inadequate: we never get to the essence, but even by our effort to make that point we reveal how much we all long for a world in which we could. Indeed, his whole project makes no sense without the implication that the struggle for understanding — understanding of a world finally beyond understanding — makes sense. Of course Derrida does not offer even a hint of any explicit salvation produced by some future cosmic fulfillment, but remember: that dream was not included in my five marks.

In recent years Derrida has dealt more and more explicitly with the contrast between the world we dream of and the world we inhabit. In his recent book, *Specters of Marx,* he dwells more than ever before on the many senses in which not just our moment in time but *the world* is "out of joint," a phrase that inescapably implies a conception of what it might be to exhibit proper jointure.[19]

Third mark: our membership in the brokenness. As users of language, which is for him all we have, human beings are revealed by Derrida as inherently, radically, permanently deficient. We are not, as the progressivists and futurists used to teach us, on an inclined plane moving upward toward full understanding: we are inherently, permanently crippled. The world of language, the gift that the nature of things has given us, has left us "originally" struggling to overcome its limitations.

In his recent work, however, Derrida has gone beyond the claim that it is our language that is inherently, "always already" in need of repair and has moved toward addressing political and moral flaws in our world. The times are out of joint not just in the traps of language but in the very existence of the injustice and misery that surround us.[20]

Which leads to the *fourth mark: responsibility to the cosmos.* As the legacy of Marx insists, he argues, we are commanded to act responsibly in the

19. Jacques Derrida, *Specters of Marx: The State of the Debt, the Work of Mourning, and the New International,* trans. Peggy Kamuf (New York: Routledge, 1994). The grappling with brokenness can be found throughout the book, but it is especially direct in chapter 1, "Injunctions of Marx."

20. See especially chapter 1, "Injunctions of Marx," where Derrida plays with Hamlet's sense that the times are out of joint, and Hamlet's sense of responsibility to do something about "righting." For example, see p. 21.

face of injustice, *to do something* about the brokenness. Derrida expresses not just a sense that "the world is out of joint" but an intense awareness of obligation, the "cursed spite," that we are "born to set it right." He attempts to set it right partly by his writing and speaking, refuting all of the nonsensical efforts of those who do not recognize their inherent brokenness, the inescapable limitations of the human use of language. But he seems now to be moving more and more to our obligation to do some actual practical fixing, overt action in the political arena.[21]

But the word "obligation" leads us once again to the *fifth mark: a faith that I do not invent the oughtness, and that therefore when there is a conflict between what I would like and what I ought to do, the ought should triumph.* The sense of obligation to set things right does not come simply from my own invention: the obligation is in — well, I would say in the nature of things. But Derrida would not use the word *nature:* he might say something like: duty is imposed by where we are, by our linguistic plight. The nature of language, of our relation to language, the history of our misstatements of that relation — all these are implicit in our very relation/non/relation to being/nonbeing/nonpresence. Cosmic reality — however chaotic — requires of us that we work at the repair job, because it is really right to do so and really wrong not to. Who has labored harder, during recent decades, to set the intellectual world right, according to his knowledge of the right?

I could wish that he did not require of us quite so much of this probing to discover the strong tension throughout his work between individual impulse and the truths of deconstructionism. But I see him as perpetually in religious tension between meanings he would personally prefer and meanings that his inquiry into his highly recondite cosmos yields. This conflict is perhaps most striking between his own sense of agency, control, authorship, and his claim that language writes him. His impulse, whenever anyone misreads him, is to claim authority and to pounce on the misreader: the difference between correct and incorrect readings is always strong. But he knows that he does not really have any ultimate authority and that he must honor that knowledge. Why? Because he *ought* to respect the knowledge of reality/non/reality that he has been pursuing.

21. References to the obligation to serve justice run throughout, but are especially strong in chapter 4, "In the Name of the Revolution, the Double Barricade (Impure 'Impure Impure History of Ghosts')."

This conviction that Derrida is a theologian in disguise was strength-ened by a brief exchange I had with him a year or so ago when he discussed this recent work, *Specters of Marx,* a work I had not then yet read. He came to Chicago to conduct a seminar on the book, which has the revealing subtitle, "The State of the Debt, the Work of Mourning, and the New International." Derrida conducted what was to me a brilliant discussion of why and how we must — follow closely now, and keep your mind on how his vocabulary resembles words used in *your* religion — how we must — *his word* (religious mark four) — if we are responsible — *his word* (mark five) — pay a debt to — *his words* (mark five) — and mourn — *his word* (marks one and two) — the spirit — *his word* — of Marx. After hearing two hours of talk about responsibilities to the dead and to the as yet unborn; about debts — *his word* — to genius — *his word;* about how we must — again *his word* (I know of no thinker who uses words like "must" and "necessarily" more freely) — recognize how the encounter with the cosmos/noncosmos he calls the abyss produces a call for "justice" — *his words* (mark four again); about how we must be humble and solicitous — *his words* (mark three); about how Marx's thought relates to Hamlet's claim that the time is out of joint — we are living in a fallen, broken world — *his words* (marks one and two); about how we can or should "learn to live finally," and "come to terms with death" — *his ethical words* — well, you see the point: his text, both in the lectures and in the book, was simply laden with religious language, with full ethical com-mands related to a mysterious unnamed commander producing what he repeatedly called "axiomatics." The study of moral commands is, as he puts it in the book's exordium, the study of "some supposedly unde-monstrable obvious fact with regard to whatever has worth, value, quality *axia* — and especially dignity."[22]

After hearing all that and more I raised my hand and asked how he would respond if someone hearing or reading him on such subjects, traditionally the subjects addressed by theologians and religious moral-ists, described him as really a believer — though he claims not to be — a disguised religious thinker, practicing a kind of theology. His first answer was that the description would be entirely false; he was not recommending any particular religion or denomination or affiliation with any church and repudiated all official denominations. When I

22. P. xx. The book is full of such language.

explained that of course I did not mean that, he said something like, "Yes, my inquiry is essentially religious — or if you prefer, theological."

Such a reply obviously would invite, in a longer study by any particularist of a given faith — Christianity, say — a detailed look at how his concerns and his way of expressing them relate to a huge range of traditional religious topics. Some Catholic particularists would want to trace, for example, how Derrida deals, openly and covertly, with the cardinal virtues and deadly sins. Where and how do prime virtues like faith, hope, and charity appear in his work? (Actually you find them everywhere — though often under synonyms and usually with less about hope than about faith and charity.) How does he deal with the cardinal sin of pride or other sins like envy, anger, and covetousness? They all crop up, though usually again under synonyms. We could turn to comparing his treatment of the dissolving manifold social self to some medieval theologians' torturous deconstruction of the soul. We could trace, as many have actually been doing, how his delicate, intricate negations as he circles the source or nonsource of language recapitulate the circlings of earlier, negative theologians as they worship the being or nonbeing beyond all negations. How does his claim that language and the life we live in it are essentially and technically *incomprehensible* relate to the frequent use of that word by medieval theologians? (See Coward, especially Derrida's reply.)

Turning back from particularist Christianity to common ground again, we might trace how his mystifying treatment of the mystery of language, his circling about meanings as if afraid to do harm by fixing them, compares with Mircea Eliade's quest through hundreds of religions for the sacred: that which must not be touched or profaned.[23] We could trace how his treatment of the gift, *la donation,* skirts the traditional ways of dealing with the one grand gratuitous gift of grace, of life itself and our gratitude to him/her/that-which-grants-it-to-us in a broken world. We could push further into his inescapable implication, at all points, that he operates within a scene, upon a stage, that he did not invent: an inherited world of interrelated signs that in its mysteries produces, indeed commands, a sustained, awe-inspired life work, lead-

23. The Mircea Eliade bibliography is immense, but a good start on his quest for the sacred can be found in his *The Sacred and the Profane: The Nature of Religion,* trans. Willard R. Trask (New York: Harcourt Brace Jovanovich, 1959).

ing the worshiper to the humble moment when, in Jerusalem, facing the obligation — again *his word* — to speak of "the trace," he decides to address these negative theologians by talking about how to avoid the profaning that is implicit in all efforts to talk about the unspeakable.[24]

None of these tracings would prove that Derrida is conducting daily worship of the divine presence he openly repudiates. But I can think of few modern authors — David Tracy, perhaps, or Paul Ricoeur or Jean-Luc Marion — who exemplify as fully as he does, in his passion for probing the deepest religious questions, the intellectual's version of daily, hourly prayer (actually it is the third of three traditional Catholic forms of prayer: meditation, contemplation). Derrida says toward the beginning of his piece on how to avoid speaking, "No, what I write is not 'negative theology.'"[25] Of course he has to say that; think of another label and it will for him not be that either. It is the ultimate in not-not-ness, because its author is the ultimate pursuer of the inadequacies of our language to pin down who we are and how we should think about the mysterious gift of finding ourselves here, wherever here is.

I do not mean to imply in all this that I think Derrida's religious/anti-religious path is the best one, or the one I myself prefer. Having begun with a reduction of life to language, defined as all we have, he will perhaps never escape the limitations imposed by that prime choice. As Richard McKeon, another great and unacknowledged deconstructionist-before-its-time, liked to insist, one's initial choices from among four elementary stuffs — whether substance, or thought, or action, or language — determine to a large degree in any inquiry where one will come out.[26] Choosing to begin with any one of those determines one's route and to some degree

24. Jacques Derrida, "How to Avoid Speaking: Denials," trans. Ken Frieden, in *Derrida and Negative Theology*, ed. Harold Coward and Toby Foshay (Albany: State University of New York Press, 1992).

25. Derrida, "How to Avoid Speaking," p. 77.

26. He usually referred to his project as "philosophical semantics," or sometimes "operationalism." In his later years he often sounded much like a Derridaian, as he would knock down one's confident assertions with "That's *entitizing*" — in other words, "You are assuming that you have hold of some undeconstructible concept or substance." The most succinct summary of his complex semantics can be found in Richard McKeon's "Philosophic Semantics and Philosophic Inquiry," in *Freedom and History and Other Essays: An Introduction to the Thought of Richard McKeon*, ed. Zahava K. McKeon (Chicago: University of Chicago Press, 1990).

simply cripples one's effort to deal with certain questions that are handled easily after beginning elsewhere.

I think Derrida would have got further faster if he had begun not with fashionable language-bound attacks on substance and foundations but, say, with an Aristotelian kind of deconstruction *and restabilization* of substantive notions; or, instead of transformations of all experience and agency into linguistic experience and nonagency, with a John Deweyan deconstruction of conceptual schemes and reestablishment of pragmatics; or, instead of a reduction of all thought into language use, a Kant-like probing of epistemological categories. Language and its deconstruction would figure in any of those enterprises, and could be pursued in ways closely akin to Derrida's. But each of them would have allowed him to arrive at his (unconscious?) religious goal somewhat less tortuously — as indeed is demonstrated by the finally religious views of Aristotle, Dewey, and Kant.

I'm afraid, however, that such a suggestion is historically absurd: he arrived at language-as-ultimate-*non*substance in the middle of a language-centered century, and it must have seemed to him simply impossible to begin with any of the other three substance-possibilities: with a mind originally steeped in the "continental," "Germanic" philosophies of his time, he "knew" that history had already exhausted those other possibilities — which, of course, it had not.

In any case, whether or not my effort to shoehorn one deconstructionist deacon into the religious camp makes sense, it seems undeniable that along with others Derrida has reestablished most if not all of the plausible rhetorical resources that too many by mid-century had thought utterly discredited. "The book" and its mysteries and paradoxes have been restored. What could be a more foundationally, essentially, groundedly religious achievement than that?

Selected Bibliography

Altizer, J. J., et al. *Deconstruction and Theology.* New York: Crossroad, 1982.

Booth, Wayne C. "Rhetoric and Religion: Are They Essentially Wedded?" In *Radical Pluralism and Truth,* edited by Werner G. Jeanrond and Jennifer L. Rike, pp. 62-80. New York: Crossroad, 1991.

Comstock, Gary L. "Two Types of Narrative Theology." *Journal of the American Academy of Religion* 55 (winter 1987).

Coward, Harold, and Toby Foshay, eds. *Derrida and Negative Theology.* Albany: State University of New York Press, 1992.

Critchley, Simon. *The Ethics of Deconstruction: Derrida and Levinas.* London: Blackwell, 1992.

Derrida, Jacques. *Specters of Marx: The State of the Debt, the Work of Mourning, and the New International.* Translated by Peggy Kamuf. New York: Routledge, 1994; originally published, Paris, 1993.

————. *A Derrida Reader: Between the Blinds.* Edited by Peggy Kamuf. New York: Columbia University Press, 1991.

————. "How to Avoid Speaking: Denials." In *Derrida and Negative Theology,* translated by Ken Frieden, edited by Harold Coward and Toby Foshay. Albany: State University of New York Press, 1992.

————. *Sauf le nom.* Paris: Galilée Press, 1993.

Detweiler, Robert, ed. "Derrida and Biblical Studies." *Semeia* 23 (1982).

Hart, Kevin. *The Trespass of the Sign: Deconstruction, Theology, and Philosophy.* Cambridge: Cambridge University Press, 1989.

Hartman, Geoffrey. *Saving the Text: Literature/Derrida/Philosophy.* Baltimore: Johns Hopkins University Press, 1981.

Holland, Scott. "How Do Stories Save Us? Two Contemporary Theological Responses." *Conrad Grebel Review* 12 (spring 1994): 131-53.

Jasper, David, ed. *Postmodernism, Literature, and the Future of Theology.* New York: St. Martin's Press, 1993.

Jeanrond, Werner. "Theology in the Context of Pluralism and Postmodernity: David Tracy's Theological Method." In *Postmodernism, Literature, and the Future of Theology,* edited by David Jasper. New York: St. Martin's Press, 1993.

Lindbeck, George. *The Nature of Doctrine: Religion and Theology in a Postliberal Age.* Philadelphia: Westminster, 1984.

Margenau, Henry, and Roy Abraham Varghese, eds. *Cosmos, Bios, Theos:*

Scientists Reflect on Science, God, and the Origins of the Universe, Life, and Homo Sapiens. LaSalle, Ill.: Open Court, 1992.

Marion, Jean-Luc. *God without Being: Hors-Texte.* Translated by Thomas A. Carlson. Chicago: University of Chicago Press, 1991.

Moore, Stephen D. *Literary Criticism and the Gospels: The Theoretical Challenge.* New Haven: Yale University Press, 1989.

Ricoeur, Paul. *Oneself as Another.* Chicago: University of Chicago Press, 1992.

Ruf, Henry, ed. *Religion, Ontotheology, and Deconstruction.* New York: Paragon House, 1989.

Schad, John. "'Hostage of the Word': Poststructuralism's Johannine Intertext." Unpublished manuscript.

Taylor, Mark C. *Deconstructing Theology.* New York: Crossroad, 1982.

Tracy, David. *The Analogical Imagination: Christian Theology and the Culture of Pluralism.* New York: Crossroad, 1981.

————. "Lindbeck's New Program for Theology: A Reflection." *Thomist* 49 (summer 1985): 460-72.

Wallace, Mark I. *The Second Naiveté: Barth, Ricoeur, and the New Yale Theology.* Macon, Ga.: Mercer University Press, 1990.

Ward, Graham. *Barth, Derrida, and the Language of Theology.* New York: Cambridge University Press, 1995.

————. "Why Is Derrida Important for Theology?" *Theology* 95 (1992).

MARK R. SCHWEHN

Christianity and Postmodernism: Uneasy Allies

❦   ❦

I

EXACTLY FOUR WEEKS AGO, I visited for the first time the University
of Virginia. There, I was privileged to deliver a brief address in the
Rotunda, a beautiful building designed by Thomas Jefferson himself
to be the architectural heart of his community of scholars, his "academical village," as he called it. The Rotunda had originally been the
university library, and it served that purpose for almost a century. Like
all visitors, I was invited to stand in the exact center of the huge circular
dome room that occupies the entire third floor. The room is encircled
by pairs of columns, spaced at regular twenty-foot intervals. Behind the
columns are alcoves that still house hundreds of books. Jefferson
deliberately placed the bookcases behind the columns in such a way
that, from the center of the room, you cannot see them.

As I stood there, I realized that I was experiencing a perfect realization
in spatial terms of the relationship between Enlightenment and tradition. If you are centered, you see only geometrical space, parceled out
into perfectly symmetrical divisions, extending in lines radiating from
the center outward in all directions, such that no matter which direction
you face, you see the same thing. Here was universal, self-sufficient,
geometrical reason at the very center of Enlightenment, literally of

Enlightenment, for directly above you as you stand at the center of the room is the oculus, the principal window of illumination. Take one step off center, however, and you see tradition, arrayed in the books that extend behind the columns. Indeed, as soon as I took one step toward the periphery, I half expected to be greeted by Alasdair MacIntyre, a bit off center to be sure, gleefully pointing to one of the rows of books as a telling reminder of the traditional character of all rationality as well as the rational character of all traditions. This now-you-see-it-now-you-don't version of the relationship between tradition and Enlightenment, between history and reason, between accumulated human wisdom and the nature of human rationality, is perhaps nowhere else as fully realized as it is in this magnificent structure at Jefferson's university.

When one contracts one's attention from traditions in general to traditions that are religious and then more particularly to the Christian tradition, the relationship between Enlightenment and tradition at Jefferson's university becomes less a matter of optical illusion and denial and more a matter of antagonism. The United States Supreme Court has on its docket this term the case of *Rosenberger v. University of Virginia.* The university administers a fund built from compulsory student fees to support a wide range of student activities. Ronald Rosenberger and other Christian students asked for a portion of this fund to support the cost of publishing *Wide Awake,* an alternative student newspaper "of philosophical and religious expression, to facilitate discussion that fosters an atmosphere of sensitivity to and tolerance of Christian viewpoints and to provide a unifying focus for Christians of multicultural backgrounds." Although the University of Virginia granted funding to 118 other groups, including the Muslim Students Association and the Jewish Law Students Association, it is claiming in this case that it denied funding to Rosenberger and others because the First Amendment's religion clause prohibits public funding of a student publication that is religious in character.[1]

Perhaps the University of Virginia also wishes to suggest, following a line of argument recently put forward by one of its most renowned

1. I am indebted to my friend and colleague Ed Gaffney, dean of the Valparaiso School of Law, for bringing this case to my attention. For Gaffney's interpretation of the case, which I draw upon here, see Edward Gaffney Jr., "At Jefferson's University," *Commonweal* (April 21, 1995): 6-7.

philosophers, Richard Rorty, that a religious newspaper designed to foster conversation is a contradiction in terms. Writing in the spring 1994 issue of *Common Knowledge,* Rorty insisted that religion everywhere and always is a "conversation stopper." Religious citizens ought to be required to restructure their arguments in purely secular terms, dropping all references to the source of the premises of these arguments. Such omissions seem to Rorty a "reasonable price to pay for religious liberty."[2]

These images and examples should remind all of us that the conflicts between religion and a certain type of Enlightenment rationalism are far from over, as many of us are inclined to think when we focus upon the congeries of movements called postmodernity. There is a direct and, in Rorty's mind at least, a self-conscious line of continuity between Jefferson and himself, between the Enlightenment and Rorty's own philosophy, between Jefferson's views of religion and the position his university is currently taking in *Rosenberger v. University of Virginia.* Indeed, on the question of whether there really is a cultural movement that is sufficiently coherent and sufficiently distinct from modernity to earn the designation "postmodernity," I am inclined (for once) to side with Rorty and Habermas among the philosophers and Anthony Giddens among the sociologists and to say that we have before us a set of movements best understood as hyper-modernism or (perhaps) the last gasps of modernity rather than as postmodernism.

Still, there are a significant number of discordant voices in our cultural conversation, and these voices represent lines of argument and assertion that are self-consciously opposed to modernity. And it is perhaps worth asking, as a way into our subject, where in the Rotunda these postmoderns would stand. Each one, we can be sure, would have a different standpoint, probably on the margins, i.e., on the periphery of the circle, each insisting upon the powers of perception and understanding peculiar to his or her particular perspective, following a line of sight that quite deliberately does not converge upon a common center but runs instead along some eccentric tangent, occasionally intersecting with other lines of sight and insight but seldom if ever inscribing with them a common pattern or project. The postmoderns would give us,

2. Richard Rorty, "Religion as Conversation Stopper," *Common Knowledge* (spring 1994): 5.

from these several standpoints, glimpses, not steady visions, provisional and sometimes playful surmises more than settled convictions.

All of them would be profoundly uncomfortable with the room itself, its geometrical perfection, its symmetries, its unified architectural ideal. Though they may appreciate it as a cultural artifact, all of them would prefer the irregular, the shapeless, and the eclectic to the clear lines and the circular perfection of the Rotunda. They would prefer to Jefferson's academical village the city that Descartes described in such negative terms in his *Discourse on the Method* as a metaphor for the accumulated traditions of the ages — jumbled, irregular, lacking design and unity, a crazy quilt of contiguous neighborhoods.

So there is indeed something new abroad in the land, call it post-modernity if you will, and our task now is to puzzle out together what we should make of it as Christians. I think we ought to be at one and the same time worried about it and informed by it. We have been and we should have been wary of Greeks bearing gifts, and we now should be equally wary of barbarians, i.e., all of those who are not Greeks, bearing gifts. Our task, in short, is to recognize both the gifts and the dangers that postmodernity brings to us, and to recognize that some-times the gifts *are* the dangers. This is a vast undertaking, and it requires most of all communal discernment. I shall nonetheless try to open up the subject by speaking first of two dangers and then, before I conclude, of several gifts.

II

The first danger seems to me the wholesale rejection of objectivity and the uncritical celebration of perspectival understanding. Since I have suggested that Christian engagement with postmodernity proceeds best through a process of communal discernment, let me proceed with this line of argument by engaging Nick Wolterstorff's discussion of the same issue in his essay "Suffering, Power, and Privileged Cognitive Access: The Revenge of the Particular" (chapter 5 in this volume, pp. 79-94).

Nick is right, I think, in his characterization of a widespread under-standing of objectivity as a Janus-faced concept, referring on the one side to being in touch with the object, with the way things are, and on the other side to being impartial, i.e., to becoming free from the distorting lenses of personal bias. Nick is also right to regard this ideal as both crippling (his word is "paraplegic") and impossible of attainment. Finally, Nick is right to celebrate the several different standpoints from which postmodernists see the world as giving them "access to realms of reality which would otherwise be extremely difficult to come by." Indeed, my imaginary postmodernists, standing around the circumference of the dome room in the Rotunda, would each see portions and features of that room that would be totally obscured from the view of the others.

But Nick's account of the possibility and importance of privileged cognitive access omits or abbreviates important features of both academic life and our ways of thinking generally that require careful attention if other Christians are to join with Nick in celebrating perspectival knowing. First of all, though Nick acknowledges more than once that our narrative identities might just as well distort as disclose aspects of reality, he says very little about how we can distinguish at any given moment whether we have an instance of the former or the latter condition — distortion or disclosure.

We need, I think, to recognize that we share with all human beings a capacity for self-transcendence; that is, an ability to bring our own narrative identities under some measure of critical scrutiny. This is perhaps part of what Nick has in mind elsewhere in his essay when he speaks of "the conviction, fundamental to Christianity, Judaism, and Islam alike, that there is more to human beings than the merely particular." I would put it *this* way: part of what it means for humankind to be fashioned in the image of God is that we are imbued with this capacity for critical self-consciousness.

That consciousness is best exercised, Nick rightfully suggests, within communities of learning that cultivate certain habits like attention and certain practices like repentance and forgiveness. Indeed, for me, the major virtue of Nick's essay is its implicit suggestion, made more through example than assertion, that the vocation of the Christian academic in the face of postmodernity is to disentangle the notion of particularist perspectives as providing privileged cognitive access from notions of metaphysical antirealism.

As Nick acknowledges, "The prevalent current argument for allowing [particularist perspectives] entrance [into the academy] is starkly political: it assumes that no one ever has any awareness of reality and argues on that ground that it would be unjustly discriminatory to exclude any perspective" (p. 91). He might have added that this post-modern position leads directly, both logically and sociologically, to tribalism, to a lack of genuine engagement and a hardening of the lines that divide human beings from one another, and finally to the argument that diversity is an end in itself rather than a means to a larger end that is connected to the pursuit of the truth of matters.

Perhaps because the intensity of my worries over these latter realities is greater even than Nick's, I have sought elsewhere to refurbish the notion of objectivity rather than to discard it altogether.[3] I think objectivity, properly refurbished, should refer neither to the notion of unmediated access to reality nor to the view that we could ever become free from bias or purified of distortions or generically human (whatever these achievements might mean). Rather, I think objectivity should refer, and to a larger extent than we realize it has always referred, to what Thomas Haskell calls "the expression in intellectual affairs of the ascetic dimension of life."

Though he ignores altogether the significance of the historical connection between asceticism and monasticism, Haskell is right, I think, in understanding ascetic practices like objectivity as "indispensable to the pursuit of truth. The very possibility of historical scholarship as an enterprise distinct from propaganda," Haskell continues,

> requires of its practitioners that vital minimum of ascetic self-discipline that enables a person to do such things as abandon wishful thinking, assimilate bad news, discard pleasing interpretations that cannot pass elementary tests of evidence and logic, and, most important of all, suspend or bracket one's own perceptions long enough to enter sympathetically into the alien and possibly repugnant perspectives of rival thinkers. All of these mental acts — especially coming to grips with a rival's perspective — require *detachment,* an undeniably ascetic capacity to achieve some distance from one's own spontaneous perceptions and convictions, to imagine how the world appears in another's eyes, to experimentally adopt perspectives that do not come naturally — in the last analysis, to develop, as Thomas Nagel would

3. Mark R. Schwehn, "The Once and Future University," *Crosscurrents* (winter 1993/94): 456-59.

say, a view of the world in which one's own self stands not at the center, but appears merely as one object among many.[4]

In brief, on my proposal, the self standing at the center of the dome room is the one who is self-deceived. Indeed, self-deception seems, upon further reflection, to be built into the very nature of this extended metaphor, which has thus far assumed that people must *stand* still, occupying forever certain fixed *standpoints*. If we once permit the metaphor to be dynamic rather than static, the one who is "objective" is the one who moves about the room, who strives, through the exercise of those virtues Nick has enumerated, to incorporate as many of the off-center perspectives as she can. This is, of course, what Nick actually *does* in his essay, as he tells us about what he has learned from reading the Scriptures as a liberation theologian or a feminist might read them, and so forth. And it is also what I strive to do as an historian.

The second danger, and it is a danger to both the well-being of the academy and to Christianity, is the postmodern notion that the quest for truth is everywhere and always a disguised quest for power and dominion. Nick also discusses this notion, and he appears initially to embrace it. I, too, embrace it in the ultimate sense that Nick does, in that I, too, believe that even our highest and best purposes are driven to some extent, given our fallen condition, by selfish interests. I, too, am something of an Augustinian, so I think that only God can know what is really in our hearts. We are strangers even to, perhaps especially to, ourselves. And of course I agree with Nick also in a more immediate and experiential sense, whenever I attend a department meeting to consider whether the department's part of the general education program should be reduced. How could I ever, in view of the conversation that invariably ensues, deny that the so-called pursuit of truth is often if not always a quest for power?

But all of this worries me too. For one thing, most of the postmodernists that I read and know do not defend the equation of the quest for truth with the quest for power in the nuanced, self-critical, and carefully qualified way that Nick does. Instead, following Foucault, whose name is invoked sooner or later in most of these discussions, postmodernists

4. Thomas Haskell, "Objectivity Is Not Neutrality: Rhetoric vs. Practice in Peter Novick's 'That Noble Dream,'" *History and Theory* 4 (May 1990): 131.

defend this equation cynically and in an altogether reductionist way in order to urge upon all of us abandonment of any pretension to the pursuit of truth whatsoever. This is what Nick refers to, as we have seen, when he notes that the current argument for admitting particularist perspectives into the academy is "starkly political." In my judgment, this is an astonishing irony. On the one hand, the university in America arguably has less power and political influence now than it has had at any time since the end of World War II; and on the other hand, at just this moment, some of its most outspoken humanists are advancing the notion that the academy's pursuit of truth is just the pursuit of power. And not, we might add, a very successful one at that.

In some postmodernist minds this equation, once established, should lead all of us to abandon truth talk altogether. To say that something is true, on this view, is at best to pay a trivial compliment and at worst to make a repressive gesture. I think Hilary Putnam, among others, is right to dismiss this proposal on the grounds that it is "simply dotty." Putnam agrees with Wolterstorff in thinking that a certain philosophical tradition, and with it a certain picture of the world, is collapsing. But, Putnam argues — and Nick's essay gives evidence that he would be in agreement here as well — that the retail collapse of certain conceptions of representation and truth that went with that picture of the world is very different from a wholesale collapse of the notions of representation and truth. In their assaults upon a "metaphysics of presence" — the view that reality dictates its own unique description — postmoderns, especially the deconstructionists among them, have ironically given to metaphysics an exaggerated importance, according to Putnam. Our language and way of life have not been destroyed by the passing of a certain world picture. We still make perfectly good sense of the idea of an extralinguistic reality that we did not create.

Putnam's own rejoinder to the postmodern invitation to regard talk of reason, justification, and truth as politically repressive is worth quoting. Such an invitation is "dangerous," says Putnam, "because it provides aid and comfort for extremists (especially extremists of a romantic bent) of all kinds, both left and right. The twentieth century has witnessed horrible events, and the extreme left and the extreme right are both responsible for its horrors. Today, as we face the twenty-first century, our task is not to repeat the mistakes of the twentieth century. Thinking of reason [and truth] as just repressive notions is certainly not going to help us do that."[5]

I indicated earlier that Nick has shown us one way that, notwithstanding his own critique of the more deeply cynical postmodern formulation of the matter, Christians can and should nevertheless construe the university as a "vast constellation of interests contesting for power." But there is yet another way that Christians can agree with those who associate truth with power, which is at one and the same time a critique of that position. I have in mind here the saying of Jesus that my father passed on to me as my confirmation text: "If ye continue in my word, then are ye my disciples indeed; and ye shall know the truth, and the truth shall make you free." For Christians, the quest for truth is bound up inextricably with discipleship, and therefore the shape of power is for them always cruciform. To put it another way, the Christian discovers truth *ambulando,* in the course of becoming what she already is, one marked with the sign of the cross. So long as Christians remember that, for disciples, power is not dominion but obedience, faithfulness, and suffering servanthood, they can rightly claim an integral connection between truth and power. This is something like what Nick says at the end of his essay when he invokes the beautiful Augustinian notion that loving the truly lovable enables knowledge.

III

Having said this much by way of suggesting some of what I take to be the most troubling features of postmodern thought for Christians, let me now revert to the autobiographical mode of disclosure that I used at the outset of this address to suggest what I take to be some possible affinities between Christianity and postmodernity. Indeed, when I encounter some of the aspects of postmodern thought, I am reminded of a remark that H. Stuart Hughes once made about Henry Adams. Hughes said that Adams "remained so old-fashioned for so long that by the end of his life he found that he was a modern." I sometimes

5. Hilary Putnam, *Renewing Philosophy* (Cambridge: Harvard University Press, 1992), pp. 124, 132-33.

think that I have remained an old-fashioned Lutheran Christian for so long that I now find myself a postmodern (though hopefully it is not yet the end of my life). This cannot be the whole truth, however, for, as you have seen, there are many aspects of postmodernity that I oppose directly — its abandonment of the quest for truth, its disparagement of the possibility of detachment, its cynical suggestions that apparent quests for truth reduce without remainder to quests for dominion and control. So you can see that, in typically Lutheran fashion, I am disposed to say to postmodernity, on theological grounds, "Yes . . . but. . . ."

Let me therefore now proceed to outline how Christianity *might* be fortified and enriched by some of the insights of postmodernity, as the Christian faith has been historically fortified and enriched, I need not remind you, by constructive engagement with its many and various cultural contexts. I begin with a section of Luther's explanation of the third article of the first creed of the church, something I memorized as a boy and have never forgotten and have, by God's grace, come to own as part of who I am. "I believe that I cannot by my own reason or strength believe in Jesus Christ, my Lord, or come to Him; but that the Holy Ghost has called me by the gospel, enlightened me with His gifts, sanctified and kept me in the one true faith. . . ."

"What does this mean?" we might now ask in a typically Lutheran way, and what might it mean for those of us who seek to explore the connections between Christianity and postmodernity? First, it means that a deep skepticism about the powers of human reason really to comprehend the divine or to come in an unaided and self-sufficient way to a knowledge of the truth of matters is a formative aspect of the Christian life. Postmodernity invites us to appreciate the radical force and implications of this attitude, and to extend it into areas where even Luther did not dare to press it, given the needs and the restrictions, the blindness and the hatreds of his own time and place.

Like Luther, we should, I think, as we become chastened by the many postmodern critiques of the so-called Enlightenment account of the powers of human reason, understand faith as "a reckless confidence in the promises of God," rather than as what faith has become for many Christians, a rational assent to the putative truth of certain propositions. But we must also extend our skepticism, through a hermeneutics of suspicion, even to those texts that we, as Christians, regard as Sacred Scriptures. So, for example, we must, as we enter the twenty-first century, abjure the anti-Judaic features of the Gospel of John and other New Testament writings and repent of the readings and the actions that have characterized much of Christendom as it has sought to persecute and sometimes to exterminate those who in one way or another were marginal to the church militant. My own preferred hermeneutical model here is the one developed by Phyllis Trible, who, following the wonderful story of Jacob's prolonged struggle with the stranger in the darkness, wrestles with the most troublesome biblical texts until they bless her. In our day and age, this mode of biblical interpretation, one that balances a hermeneutic of suspicion with a hermeneutic of trust, should, I think, be preferred to Luther's reading of the whole of the Scriptures through the rubrics of law and gospel.

And *I* at least must go further still. I must extend this hermeneutics of suspicion to the very words of Luther I quoted. So, for example, those words "one true faith" seem deeply suspicious, taken, as they must be, within the context of Luther's attitudes toward (to take just two groups) the Anabaptists and the Jews. I must, in other words, strive to read these words as a Jew or an Anabaptist might read them, and I must, having sought to do that, admit that the word "one" here is and has been historically pernicious and often fatal. Indeed, I believe that the most Christian thing that all of us Christians can do as we enter the twenty-first century is to modify or drop altogether the exclusivist claims of Christianity. Postmodernity can help us do that, I think, both because a postmodern reading of the Scriptures can help us understand how and why these claims arose in the first place, and because, as almost any postmodern would be quick to point out, they are to some extent at odds with the deepest meaning of the gospel itself. Christians should come, in other words, on the one hand to suspect the exclusivist claims of Christianity and on the other hand to trust the unfathomable dimensions of God's love and mercy.

Second, we should as Christians, along with many postmoderns, recognize how frail and feeble are the powers of argument and analysis in a world torn by enormous hatreds, many of them religious hatreds, and no small number of these latter fueled by the energies of those who call themselves Christian. This does not simply mean reiterating Newman's wonderful insight that "keen and delicate instruments of human knowledge and human reason" cannot contend unaided against "those giants, the passion and the pride of man." It means as well that we present our arguments about how human beings should live and what should be the grounds of their hope quietly and steadily in the way we live, in the shape of our stories, in those practices, habits, and virtues that show forth the glory of God in the world. All of us here must ponder anew the striking fact that those Christians who are most welcome without question or suspicion everywhere in the world are the ones who are short on doctrinal propositions and theological verbiage and long on service to neighbors in need. I am thinking here of those very groups that Luther himself persecuted, like the Mennonites.

Third, since most of us are teachers and scholars, we must hear again, with ears attuned in part by postmodernity, the suggestion that we are finally enlightened by the gifts of the spirit. Is there any more coherent and persuasive account abroad in the land of how we can learn anything at all, of how our teaching sometimes really does result in learning? The myriad accounts offered by postmodernists about the relations between words and things, signs and referents, language and extralinguistic reality, even if we wish, as I would, to reject most of them, should have at least made us ponder anew how difficult it is to believe any purely naturalistic account of how human beings grow to speak, to understand one another, and to grow intellectually, morally, and spiritually.

We might recall and then retrieve Saint Augustine's early dialogue "On the Teacher," which begins with an elaborate and surprisingly postmodern-sounding account of the relationship between language and reality and concludes by arguing that the only real teacher is Christ or the *logos.* "We seek knowledge," Augustine wrote, "not from the speaker outside of ourselves but from the truth within that governs our mind, while the words, perhaps, prompt us to seek advice. And he to whom we go for aid is the teacher, Christ, who is said to dwell in the innermost human being, the inalterable strength and eternal wisdom of God."[6]

Fourth, the postmodern confusions about the problem of identity — the disposition in some quarters to deny the continuity of selfhood and so to dissolve notions of individual responsibility altogether and in other quarters to defend an identity politics based on accidents of ethnicity — gender, and class, should lead us to explore anew as Christians the meaning and the significance of our baptismal identities. Christians

6. Augustine, "On the Teacher," trans. Joel Lidow, in *Plato's Meno,* ed. Malcolm Brown (Indianapolis: Bobbs-Merrill, 1971), pp. 81-82.

cannot, I think, remain seriously Christian and at the same time believe that they created themselves, that they make their worlds at will. And Christians have an account of identity as something conferred, not by accidents of birth or effort of will, but sacramentally, as the spirit moves upon the face of the waters of baptism.

This account of identity is both very old, arising as it did in the practices of the ancient church, and very new in that, like postmodernity, it challenges all endeavors to render a complete account of human identity in strictly naturalistic terms, and construes it instead in narrative terms that are both highly particular and quite universal. Even as the baptized one is given a particular name, she is marked with the sign of the cross and so received into the body of Christ, making his story her own. Indeed, "we are buried with Christ by baptism unto death that like as he was resurrected by the glory of the Father, even so we also shall walk in newness of life."

IV

We might ask in concluding whether these scattered suggestions about the uneasy and partial alliances that might be provisionally made between Christianity and postmodernity really add up to anything coherent and important for the Christian life. Not quite, I think — yet there is one proposal that gathers up and thematizes a number of them into a model of Christian discipleship that seems to me most appropriate to the twenty-first century. Let me propose in closing, then, that the encounter between Christianity and postmodernity might eventuate in a preference for the Marcan view of the Christian life over the Johannine view that the church catholic has preferred for some twenty centuries now.

John's Gospel begins with a very modernist-sounding hymn to the preexistent *logos* and ends with several post-resurrection appearances to satisfy logical positivists like Thomas who seek empirical verification for all knowledge claims. Mark's Gospel begins with the conferral upon Jesus of a baptismal identity that he withholds from his followers for most of his life, and it ends with an empty tomb. John gives us the high Christology of a Jesus in control of his own destiny from beginning to end; Mark gives us the sometimes fearful, often secretive, harried man whom God finally raised up. John's Jesus asks only rhetorical questions;

Mark's Jesus asks genuine questions and is filled with doubts. Mark's Jesus shows us how to act in the midst of a hostile and uncomprehending empire on the brink of ruin, and it teaches us to expect betrayal and a sense of abandonment even by God and the angels. Mark gives us a world where everything happens "immediately" and where we get at best a now-you-see-it-now-you-don't view, not of the traditional character of Enlightenment, but of the presence of the kingdom of God on earth.

In short, Mark gives us a postmodern world, as some critics who are friendly to postmodernism like Frank Kermode have rightly understood. In that world Jesus is, as we have seen, the model disciple and we are the real disciples — Peter, James, John, and the rest. And we turn out to be dolts, fearful people who seldom recognize the truth, who glimpse it only fitfully, and who are prepared to abandon it at a moment's notice. We fail to get the parables. We completely fail to understand the nature of Jesus' power, since we are determined to fit him into a preestablished story line or into our own theological and hermeneutical categories. We try our best, but we just never manage on our own, and we remain afraid to the very end of the story, contemplating the meaning of an empty tomb. But it is this very absence and this very silence that finally enable even us dolts to discern the presence that once walked among us.

Had we ever tried, in Mark's world — our postmodern world — to see Jesus from the vantage points of those positioned on the margins, like the nameless servants, the despised centurion, and a few women, some named, some not named, we just might have seen Jesus as the Christ, the anointed one who must die. Elizabeth Fiorenza has helped all of us to see that the person who saw most clearly the truth of the Christ and who bore witness to that truth most effectively was an anonymous female character who said nothing at all. No propositions. No arguments. A liturgical gesture. An act of worship. An anointing. It was Jesus rather who spoke: "She has done what she could; she has anointed my body beforehand for burying. And truly, I say to you, wherever the gospel is preached in the whole world, what she has done will be told in memory of her."

She was, I think, the first postmodern Christian. Go and be thou likewise.

PART FOUR

Strangers, Friends, and New Communities

PAULA P. BROWNLEE

"I Was a Stranger and You Welcomed Me": Bridging between Languages

ALL OF US bring to this volume particular perspectives from which we desire to explore the intersection of Christianity and contemporary culture. Most of the other participants bring perspectives from their scholarly work in either religion or other fields in the humanities. My own background is so different that I feel the need to lead off with some description of it, if only to set the stage for your expectations for my comments. In some respects I may be a stranger to this company, yet I have not wanted to remain so. I hope that I can represent a view of others in the communities of our campuses, and at least some in the communities of our churches, who also often feel like strangers — and who also do not want to remain so. What may be the nature of this "strangeness," why should we care, and what are some of the actions we may take?

As I wrote these words, without yet the benefit of becoming acquainted with the participants, I drew conclusions from what I knew of the speakers. Their titles reinforced my sense of colleagues who easily understand each other's language of discourse, while I may not. They may disagree, but much of the actual language would be familiar among them. For me to enter such a gathering and contribute something to the discussion is difficult. I shall stray far from our overall title, "Christianity and Culture in the Crossfire." You might guess that "crossfire" is not a metaphor I warm to, and maybe I do not very well perceive it, even having heard the discussion of battle, fighting, and war. For me, the fighting sounds are faint and far away; as I hear it, between Christianity and culture there is more an anxious, vast silence than a raging battle. It is important to be sure that the views of many, many others in the academy who also are committed Christians of various traditions are included in our thinking. For some of us, there is no easy bridging between our academic and religious lives. The languages are too different. The worlds lie apart.

I still describe myself as a chemist, because I was formed intellectually and worked long years in that discipline. Alongside that I identify myself as an active Episcopalian, though a questing one, delighted with the notion of the communal body, less excited by the actuality of the congregations I know and have known. On the one hand, the congregations that I have been part of have not made space for intellectual enquiry. On the other, chemists on campus do not often find themselves debating religious questions! Here I would like to add the question that Jean Hampton asked in her essay. In "fighting" for a position that makes room for a reality that "naturalists" deny, she says:

> Some Christians I know in the academy have decided not to fight at all. They worship privately and philosophize publicly in a way that is respectful of science, albeit not worshipful of it. Their respect is, in my view, legitimate. Yet not to stand up for a moral and religious reality that one believes in is a kind of quiet betrayal of those realities. So in my view one has to stand up for that reality. How does one do it, and do it effectively?[1]

My current professional work is centered at the Association of American Colleges and Universities — the association in Washington which focuses on strengthening and promoting liberal education on our nation's campuses. On many of the campuses where liberal learning is highly valued, religion is not considered an essential part of a full liberal education. If a contemporary definition of liberal education includes the concept of integrating understanding from many fields into the

---

1. Jean Hampton, "Feminism, Moral Objectivity, and Christianity," chapter 7 in this volume, at p. 115.

building of a whole life, then the omission of religion is odd. From an interested layperson's view of matters religious and spiritual, I note the almost total silence on these matters in thoughtful campus discourse — and I feel a separation of my commitments. Faculty and deans who espouse the values of liberal education are contending always, equivalently, with the separateness of the disciplines. I believe that on most campuses there is in actuality much more silence and separation than dispute between "warring parties."

We are all aware of the chasms of misunderstanding that can exist between people of different faiths. I have been saddened to realize just how wide are the separations also between academics in different disciplines. Any faculty member who has ever served on a tenure and review committee knows well how impenetrable a field distant from one's own can seem. Lack of understanding had seemed to me to be the cause. Ultimately, the result of such lack of understanding of colleagues' work would usually be withdrawal, perhaps with a shrug. I only fairly recently experienced, in contrast, the powerful emotion that can be evoked by such incomprehension. I was attending an ARIL (Association of Religion in Intellectual Life) Consultation — a three-day conference of about one hundred participants. The theme was "Faith That Works," and six substantial papers were presented by scholars in very different fields. They had been encouraged to be as personal as they wished in discussing the ways in which their faith intersected with the intellectual work of their lives. Most chose to read very scholarly papers. The scientist, for example, spoke from his perspective (lucidly and powerfully, I thought). While I may not have agreed with all he said, I admired the way he crafted his arguments and marshaled the evidence. On the other hand, the linguistic philosopher lost me. I had read the paper beforehand and thought I understood much of it, finding it "interesting." As I listened, I was puzzled: why couldn't I understand what the paper was saying? Then I found it increasingly obscure, and boredom set in. Not much later, I found myself getting angry, and I actually ended up feeling furious, and excluded. I could not believe the depth of my own anger. Later, I heard others expressing delight with this paper, and with the scientist's paper, outrage. The same one I had found so lucid! Other papers angered or pleased other participants. The dividedness was not on matters of faith traditions or even religious belief, but on incomprehension of others' intellectual fields.

The intensity of emotion generated by papers that each of us felt we should have been able to understand was a revelation to me. I was so taken aback that I have spoken often since of our need to learn to write in publicly accessible language — within the academy, as well as for a larger public. Chemists feel alienated by talk of deconstructionism and postmodernist criticism. Artists wonder about fractals and chaos theory. There is little bridging language between disciplines in the academy. Among the many languages of different religious traditions, we can note as examples: the use of silence by Quakers, the passionate language of evangelical Christians, and the liturgical and doctrinal terms of Catholicism. These languages are shared within each faith tradition; they form divides between even those who call themselves Christian.

I believe then that we need to recognize first the many boundaries of disciplines and of religious belief which make us profoundly strangers to each other. The metaphor of welcoming the stranger represents a strong vision of what higher education and liberal learning should be about. How much more should those of us who live fragmentedly in two worlds — in academia and in religious community — work to bring the two worlds together into discourse.

"I was a stranger and you welcomed me." In the act of welcoming we can imagine the joy of the one welcomed, alongside the enrichment of the one doing the welcoming. The former stranger, once included, can progress from being visitor, through acquaintance, to friend, and if joining a group, member. It goes without saying that the stranger needs to want to be included, to be freed from the descriptor "stranger" which is altogether an unwanted status. The stranger had had to signal a willingness to be welcomed, an openness to the "other" or community of interest. Returning to consider again our academic communities, made up of departments of colleagues: how well do faculty at our own small colleges, let alone universities, interact across their diversity? And for denominational colleges, many of which are now far down the road to becoming largely "secular," how easily do faculty bring together their commitments to discipline, to liberally educating students from many majors and interests, and to their religious tradition? A friend of mine recently wrote to me, upon returning from a Lilly conference: "The church-related colleges have . . . to attempt, through religion, to define a conception of the good life that is not wholly or primarily material, and the history of liberal education shares that latter concern." How well do we really find our voices?

Alas! for a multitude of possible reasons, I believe that few of us bring together, at any one time, all the fragments of the interests, let alone passions, of our lives. We are too careful, too cautious, and perhaps have been made shy by earlier experience. The result adds up to too much silence, a lack of questioning, or misunderstanding. We don't often dare to say we don't know the terms of the discussion, or that we wish you would translate your peculiar jargon into everyday English.

Why should we care that academic and religious communities are so fragmented and so separated? Each needs to teach so much to and learn so much from the other. We could replace the distressing picture of "anti-intellectual churches" and "antireligious colleges and universities" with a vision of intellectually lively, inclusive churches — and colleges and universities where religious issues are debated as freely and thoughtfully as any other issues. And above all, our vision must include our students in the center, questioning, learning, and challenging. I was so happy with Nick Wolterstorff's comment that we need to find a different kind of rudder than only the classical philosopher's. He included the expressions of narrative, wit, passion, and the need to speak and hear. I add again, we can only hear those who speak in language we can understand. In addition, Miroslav Volf called up our need for imagination in order to communicate.

The building of communities of enquiry may seem easily attainable. After all, colleges and universities were designed to develop so, and Christian belief includes some level of commitment to the church as the mystical body of Christ. Perhaps it is the very assumption of intellectual or Christian community at the center of our organizations that has clouded our awareness of the actual lack of community across the divides of which I have been speaking. One of the most poignant personal accounts of this realization was written by Jane Tompkins, professor of English at Duke University. Her 1992 article in *Change* magazine is full of insights and longing, as she returned to her university after a sabbatical year at the National Humanities Center, where she had experienced "the ideal combination of society and solitude." She goes on to ask, "Why shouldn't there be an atmosphere of camaraderie, opportunities for companionship alternated with solitude in the course of the normal university day?" She identifies what she is looking for: "a common enterprise; belonging; good feelings in the workplace; a community of hope; an integrated life." She ends her article, after identifying some of the barriers to achieving such community, with the inclusion of students. "Universities, it seems to me, should model something for students besides an ideal of individual excellence — the Olympic pole-vaulter making it over the bar. They should model social excellence as well as personal achievement. . . ."[2]

Once we can envision the community of enquiry we desire, building it will require active engagement, demanding time and energy. How many discussion groups and small communities of purpose are started with enthusiasm, only to founder on the shoals of competing time-demands? To become a reality, the vision must be compelling, enthusiastic leadership present, and the continuing, unfolding community seen as a moving, not static, enterprise. It must be worth the precious time given to it. In describing the development of a new curriculum at a member institution, the following words were used: "There's a tremendous difference between talking about what needs to be done and doing it." Doing demands precious time. Those words are pertinent to us, at this conference.

A conference of interested and interesting people, with papers to read and debate in which to engage, is, at the time, a valuable experience. Too often, however, the learning stays with the individual only, or at best with his or her close professional colleagues and students. I am privileged to be invited to a number of conferences in a year. Recently there have been several devoted to such vast themes as reinventing the research university, rethinking liberal education, or reengineering the academic institution. People with high responsibilities gather at these conferences, exchange ideas, and depart. While we can never tell where one good idea may spark a whole succession of events that could lead to actual work on one or many campuses, I worry at the lack of intentional force toward turning "thought into action." Incidentally, at one of these recent conferences, the one on "reinventing the research university," the colleagues invited to attend included only *one* person from the humanities, and I was the only person speaking to the breadth of learning essential to the education of undergraduates in such settings. Everyone else was either a scientist or an engineer. This illustrates the isolation we have perpetuated between the fields. Perhaps we have not even noticed!

2. Jane Tompkins, "The Way We Live Now," *Change* 24, no. 6 (November-December 1992): 12-18.

I believe that we have an opportunity here to take our knowledge and apply it in most valuable ways. How can you, who are well versed in speaking to each other about your field and, I assume, about various kinds of religious experience including your own, help others out of their silence? On our campuses, and even in our churches, most people in fields other than religion have placed religious questions firmly into their private, personal lives. Religion is largely separate from public intellectual debate. How have we come to such a state of affairs, and how may we move to a new level of open discussion?

Beyond these questions lies the equally important challenge of "translating" the specialized language of the various humanities fields into narrative comprehensible to other academics and educated laypersons. Is it possible to transmit everything — from the broadest new concepts to the more difficult and refined intricacies — in simple language? Maybe Schweitzer's description of Goethe's use of simple language can inspire us: "He possesses the secret of a painter of words as he brings to our imagination the visions that come into his own. Further, he does not express himself in sonorous language overlaid with the glitter of adjectives, but in the simple, sober language of everyday life, which he knows how to lift to the rank of poetry."[3]

In my own experience, a great deal of the theoretical and experimental work in chemistry can be explained and made interesting to all kinds of people, if the people are interested to know. After all, in teaching undergraduates, we work hard to do this all the time. Admittedly, before early initiates can join a debate, greater knowledge must be acquired. But there are many stages between full inclusion and total exclusion. For ourselves, better that at least the terms of the debate be understood as a starting point. Then gradually, strangers from all sides will be able to be included in the community of enquiry, thereby greatly enriching all experience.

Talking again about undergraduates, they are given few opportunities even to hear vigorous discussion by professionals, let alone to begin to edge into the discussion, as they are able. I recently heard someone use the expression that in our colleges we "infantilize our students." I was immediately horrified, and yet as I thought about it, I realized sadly

3. Albert Schweitzer, *A Reflection on the Greatness of Goethe*, pamphlet, privately printed.

that it may be partly true. Our students also let themselves be so treated. It is time we treated them with the expectation that they have become young adults of intelligence, ready to test the waters of junior colleague-ship.

I have been candid about my initial apprehension about participating in this project. I believed myself to be too much the "stranger" to the language in which the intersection of Christian commitment and intellectual enquiry would be explored. Yet, as an active member of ARIL, I was glad to foretell the community of interest between us here. ARIL, among other activities, has been working for several years to set up campus groups that engage this same intersection. But it is slow and difficult work. I wondered if my individual participation would be anything more than marginal. The answer is, of course, no — you have indeed welcomed this stranger — on this occasion. But there are still many, many others also who need to be welcomed to the discourse in new ways. To achieve this goal, we shall have to work together to uncover new language that includes us all.

DENNIS O'BRIEN

Authors and Authority:
A Catholic Reflection

🐚   🐚

SHORTLY BEFORE I went to the University of Rochester, there was a heated debate in the faculty of Arts and Science about creating a department of religion. One of the most distinguished members of the philosophy faculty expressed his exasperation at the very idea. "If we have a department like *that*," he declared, "the next thing you know we will be teaching witchcraft." At which the chair of the department of anthropology rose and said, "We already do!"

I take my theme from this noteworthy example of faculty debate. How is it that our universities, founded and fostered by the church of the Middle Ages, and our colleges founded by so many fervent Christian denominations, should seem such unlikely places for the study of religion that the best we can hope for is being tucked into a course on totem and taboo? The answer: a profound change in the very idea of the university, a change which inherently rejects biblical claims.

How did this change occur? Who is to blame? The change occurred relatively recently — 1614 to be exact. And we should blame the Jesuits. Why not? They have been blamed for worse things than causing the modern university!

Sixteen fourteen was the graduation year of the most famous and influential product of Jesuit education ever — and a very disgruntled graduate at that. I give you his assessment of his course of studies.

I had an extreme desire to acquire instruction. But as soon as I had achieved the entire course of instruction, I entirely changed my opinion. For I found myself embarrassed with so many doubts . . . that it seemed to me that the effort to instruct myself had no other effect than . . . increasing my own ignorance. And yet I was studying at one of the most celebrated Schools in Europe.[1]

The disappointed graduate was René Descartes; the "celebrated School" was the Jesuit college at La Flèche. Descartes was so disappointed with his Jesuit education that he went out and invented the modern world and the modern university all by himself. Given the state of both, one could wish that the Jesuits had been more persuasive.

The central insight of this brilliant Frenchman governs the modern university to this very day. What Descartes rejected at La Flèche was the then-basic *method* of university study: the reliance on authorities for truth. The scholastic tradition was forever appealing to the fathers of the church, the works of Plato and Aristotle, the preeminence of Aquinas or Suárez. But the authorities seemed to disagree, they weren't clear, they failed to prove their points scientifically. The only thing that really impressed Descartes in his schooling was mathematics, and that method would be his key to truth. This powerful and effective "mathematical" mind-set has dominated science, society, and the schools ever since.

I remind you of Descartes's approach to truth: he said to himself, let's suppose that everything I have ever believed is false — or at least doubtful. (Most of us have retail doubts; Descartes was in the wholesale end of the business.) He started off doubting easy stuff like optical illusions; then he wondered whether everything was only the illusion of a dream; and finally, how did he even know that he had a body — perhaps he was a brain being programmed by an evil genie or a computer with a Pentium chip. As every survivor of Philosophy 101 knows, Descartes finally concluded that there was at least one thing that he did know for sure — he was thinking, and as long as he was thinking he wasn't a nothing. *Cogito, ergo sum:* I think, therefore I am. It is surely the most famous single saying in the philosophical literature.

"I think, therefore I am." What's wrong with that? If Descartes was

1. René Descartes, *Discourse on the Method,* pt. 1 (London: J. M. Dent and Sons, 1912), p. 5.

a thinking thing, aren't colleges and universities preeminently thinking places? Recall Descartes's doubts and dilemmas. He worried about sticks that appeared bent in water, about evil demons and that life may be a programmed dream. In dreams I have a delusory history in a delusory body. Descartes will not be fooled; he says he can do without the hypothesis of body and history. Pure thought needs neither. I will be a thinking thing — *just* a thinking thing!

You need not spend ten minutes on a contemporary campus to discover the problem with Descartes's thinking thing. What gender, what color, what ethnic history does this thinking thing have? For Descartes, thinking things are disembodied: no gender, no color, no historical cults or cultures. It fits the mathematical model. Nothing could be more true, certain, universal — and disembodied — than algebra. Only thinking that approaches that lofty level will be admitted to the academy.

Descartes's ideal has become the dominant university tradition: the "pure" scientific intellect, the detached observer, who proves hypotheses and comes to truth. It is the model of modernity's greatest invention: natural science. It was to that tradition that my philosophical colleague appealed in his animadversion against religion in the curriculum. Since the rise of the "research university" paradigm for higher education in the late nineteenth century, the scientific cast of mind would appear wholly to have dominated responsible scholarship.

No one, least of all myself, would say one word against the grandeur of the sciences. Modern science is one of the great triumphs of humanity, and if Descartes is its prophet — as he surely is — let him take the praise. But if the university is Cartesian, what can we do with the demands on our campus today for hearing embodied voices — voices which should be barred de jure from the palace of pure Cartesian thought?

If we are wholly committed to the vision of the detached observer, then reattaching our inquiry to earth and history seems to lead only to passionate relativism and ultimate skepticism. We will be as full of doubts at the end of our education as Descartes found himself after graduation from La Flèche. This is not a pointless fear. It is entirely possible to regard the university as a collection of cults, each with its own special truth known only to those of special birth or background. One replaces the detached observer with a pantheon of faiths and frenzies. Deconstructionism replaces Descartes's austere quest with Derrida's "dance of innumerable choreographies."

It is more than fashionable for postmodernists to bash Descartes. The transcendent Cartesian thinking intellect is labeled the "view from nowhere" and is to be replaced by the passionate, embodied voice of my race, my sex, my faith and family. But as Susan Bordo has pointed out, the "deconstructionist" voice, the "dance of innumerable choreographies," is no better than the old transcendent. Derrida's "deconstructionist" self is the "shape-shifter," the "trickster" who is now this, now that: "tis here, tis there, tis gone" like Hamlet's father's ghost.[2] It is not clear that either the transcendent or the trickster can give *authority* to my voice as woman or man, or African or Asian. If Descartes's detachment and Derrida's dance *both* fail to ground discourse in earth, and history, the problem of an authoritative embodied voice remains a problem to be solved. Perhaps we can find a solution — or the start of a solution — in the "method of authority" which Descartes so grandly abjured.

The clamor of embodied voices on the contemporary campus, whether in student protest or professorial hermeneutics, is a return of sorts to a method of authority; it is a demand for "authors." The modern cry is "Author! Author!" *Authors* come in very specific voice, often as male or female, black or white, Asian or European, Elizabethan or Victorian. George Eliot is clearly a British female voice of the Victorian period — even if she chose a masculine nom de plume.

Which leads me back to La Flèche and its worthy predecessors. Insofar as these were Christian universities, they were founded on authorship or "authority." The Christian claim echoes the demand of ardent feminists and outraged ethnics: there is a particular, embodied history which is authoritative. It was deeply offensive to the intellectual tradition of the ancient world to claim that there was some special value in the specific history of the Jewish people and Jesus of Nazareth. The great apostate emperor Julian saw the issue clearly when he decried the parochialism of biblical religion in the face of the grand cosmopolitanism of Rome. "Reason enables us to attain a knowledge of the divine

---

2. Susan Bordo, "The View from Nowhere and the Dream of Everywhere: Heterogeneity, Adequation, and Feminist Theory," *APA Newsletter on Feminism and Philosophy* 88 (March 1989): 2.

essence quite independently of any disclosures on the part of Moses, Jesus, or Paul. [The God of the Bible is] short sighted, resentful, capricious, sectional and particularist. . . ."[3]

"Short sighted, resentful, capricious . . . particularist" — sounds like my kind of guy! I can identify with that sort of a God, while the "divine essence" of Julian leaves me cold. Julian's rational cosmopolitanism recoils from Christian particularism in the same terms we often hear for rejecting gender, race, or ethnic claims made on the contemporary curriculum.

But if biblical religion rests on particular history, on the authority of specific voices, it is necessary to make a few theological remarks about the notion of "authority" — at least as I understand it in the biblical tradition. What exactly is the "authority" attributed to the Bible or to Jesus?

There are Christian believers who would say that Christian truth is quite on a par with scientific truth — it is just that some truths are proved by reason and experiment, others we have to take on authority. I have never seen heaven, so I must rely on the report of someone who has; I've never been to the moon, so I have to rely on Buzz Aldrin. "Only the Son knows the Father," so we rely on Jesus to tell us about the divine.

I do not believe that this can be the sense in which Jesus is "authoritative." Jesus is not an authoritative informant, he is a savior. It is not in his telling us about heavenly truths that he is so special: if he were to do that he would have been a prophet. Muhammad is the "seal of the prophets" delivering a divine vision, but the last thing that a Muslim will claim is that Muhammad is a savior. Christianity is not the revelation *of* Jesus, it is the revelation *in* Jesus. "He who believes in *me* shall never die." If you accept this distinction, then the sense of Jesus as *authority* is utterly different from the authority of Buzz Aldrin as the only one who has seen the moon. It just happens to be the case that Buzz Aldrin has been there, but if Wayne Booth or Jack Neusner get there, they are just as good witnesses as Buzz. I don't think Christians believe Jesus is replaceable even by these two worthy scholars! It is not the teachings of Jesus that make him special — it is life, death, and

---

3. C. N. Cochrane, *Christianity and Classical Culture* (New York: Oxford University Press, 1957), p. 266. Cochrane is summarizing from Julian's *In Galileos*.

resurrection that caused his followers to form a cult of the person Jesus whom they declared the Christ of God. Jesus does not deliver God's word as Muhammad delivers the word of Allah. Jesus is, in Karl Rahner's phrase, the unsurpassable word of God.

Walker Percy said Judaism and Christianity are not members in good standing of the world's great religions. What he meant is that they do not offer spiritual wisdom as does the Buddha or Lao-tzu. The biblical religions are an ongoing life: the ongoing life of the Jewish people, the ongoing life of Jesus in the community of those who take his life as unsurpassable. Franz Rosenzweig puts the Jewish claim powerfully:

> The belief [of a Jew] is not the content of a testimony, but rather the product of a reproduction. The Jew, engendered by a Jew, attests his belief by continuing to procreate the Jewish people. His belief is not in something: he is himself the belief.[4]

"[The Jew] is himself the belief," and Jesus says, "He who believes in me." I don't want to get any deeper into the theological tangle which these claims would raise, I only want to state that the *authority* of the Jewish experience and of Jesus for Christians is not primarily some sort of special knowledge, wisdom, or testimony which can be separated from an embodied ongoing life. In the academic context, "authority" is always theoretically replaceable: Paula Brownlee may go to the moon. In the biblical tradition, a particular life cannot be replaced by another life.

Let me place this biblical embodied voice within the academic problems of multiculturalism. If one accepts the irreplaceability of the embodied reality of Jesus, then it is clear that a Transcendent Cartesian Ego cannot be the self addressed by the biblical tradition. It is also clear that the Shape Shifter Self can't be addressed: he, she, them is/are too evanescent. If the campus dilemma of multiculturalism is the dichotomy between the universal transcendent self and the relativistic, embodied self, the biblical voice is unusual — if not downright contradictory: it is embodied and yet claims to be universally authoritative — neither slave nor free, male nor female, Greek nor Jew. Jesus is the unsurpassable word.

4. Franz Rosenzweig, *The Star of Redemption,* trans. W. H. Wallo (New York: Holt, Rinehart & Winston, 1970), p. 342.

How can Christianity claim to be both "particularist" and "universal"? It is important to avoid the ever-available Cartesian model. One might regard Christian truth like the rational concept that lies above all the varieties of specific utterance. English "chair" is French *"chaise"* is German *"Stuhl."* There is a common concept up there above the linguistic variations — particularly if one is being "scientific." In biology, a rose is *le rose* is *die Rose,* but Gertrude Stein was wrong when it came to authored texts. Whatever the "universality" of meaning that is effected by the biblical story, it is not the abstract truth behind all the cultural clothing. I have always thought it significant that in the story of Pentecost, the foreigners assembled heard the message "each in his own tongue." They didn't suddenly come to understand Aramaic — or whatever the apostles preached in — but the message came in the deepest cultural voice: their own tongues.

To address the dilemma of particular and universal, let me adopt a lesson from Henry James. In the preface of *The Spoils of Poynton,* James tells how that novel emerged. He was attending a fashionable London affair and heard a story about a complex inheritance matter in the north. Suddenly he saw what he called "the germ," the nugget of complications which was to become the full-scale novel. As the person at the party continued the actual history, it turned out very differently than James's novel and quite unsuitable for the artist's purposes. Here is James's comment:

> Life being all inclusion and confusion, and art being all discrimination and selection, the latter in search of the hard latent *value* with which it is concerned . . . the artist finds in his tiny nugget washed free of awkward accretions and hammered into sacred hardness the very stuff for a clear affirmation . . . for the indestructible. At the same time, it amuses him again and again to note how, beyond the first step of the actual case . . . life persistently blunders and deviates, loses herself in the sand. The reason, of course, is that life has no direct sense of the subject and is capable, luckily for us, of nothing but splendid waste.[5]

Suppose that the biblical story is something like James's "germ," a set of revelatory conditions and circumstances with which humans write

5. Henry James, *The Spoils of Poynton* (New York: Scribner, 1908), pp. v-vi.

out the story of life. (Northrop Frye develops an analogous thesis when he regards the Bible as "the Great Code" which underlies the many stories of Western literature.) Christians and Jews hold the biblical story to be "authoritative," the germ of the various "stories" of life. The biblical story is *the* germ, but only the germ: it is not the embodied story which is developed in my life as a man, yours as a woman, his as a black, across the particular cultures and individual experiences of the race.

A further — and radical — departure from James: James is talking about "art." Art is like a luminous Platonic form: hard, golden, clear, and indestructible. In contrast, life is all "inclusion and confusion" with no "direct sense of the subject," capable of only "waste." Biblical religion is the germ of actual life, not the shapely plot of novels. James himself notes that "luckily" life does not develop like art and is capable only of waste — but he says *"splendid* waste."

Biblical religion exists not as art but in James's domain of "waste." Whether it is splendid or not is *the* religious issue. The Christian germ of a story deals with a life which is hardly a "work of art" but full of confusions, blunders, loss, betrayal, rejection, death — waste. But the Christian will proclaim that this life of Jesus was a "splendid waste," a life which in its "waste" is one that I can take as the germ of my own life and find it "splendid." In Sartre's *Nausea,* the protagonist finds life "too much" an obscene overflow in contrast to the gemlike purity of art. What Sartre's atheism perceives as nauseous and too much, the saint perceives as the overflowing glory of God. Waste or splendor lies in the beliefs of the beholder.

The biblical germ relates, then, to all our embodied stories. Carlyle said history is the essence of innumerable biographies. I don't know about history, but I think biblical religion is the essence of innumerable biographies as they are developed with even more than Jamesian subtlety from the biblical "germ."

Christianity would claim to be the germ of many voices, the unsurpassable word which reveals the harmonies and creative dissonances of the great world rumble of cries, protests, exultations, and affirmations. What would such a claim mean within the academic context? To insist in a university that there is *some* unsurpassable code, germ, or voice should be an inherent principle since the *search* for such a voice is the fundamental demand for communication over cult. To claim that the

Christian voice is central is, in turn, hardly the fashion of the hour. The legitimacy for organizing the conversation of humanity around any "fundamental" voice can be given at least plausibility by time and tradition. It is not insignificant, then, that there are Christian colleges like this one linked to two thousand years of tradition in philosophy, art, moral insight, and spirituality. Who knows, maybe in two thousand more years there will be Crystal Universities meditating over Shirley MacLaine. But I doubt it.

Every university should *seek* for an unsurpassable voice, it should demand communication — not to dissolve voices but to demand that they share their insights into the human condition. But again, communication among cultures does not aim at some cultural Esperanto. If there is an unsurpassable word, it will be heard by each in his and her own language.

The Christian claim moves a step beyond the *academic search* for some unsurpassable voice because it asserts that the word has *already* been spoken. To believe that the unsurpassable word has already been uttered, whether in Torah, Christ, the Buddha, in the Qur'an — or by Wittgenstein — goes against the academic grain with its everlasting inquiry and openness to new truth. All well and good, and yet there is something deeply troubling about applying this legitimate academic openness to the dialogue of voices that I have been describing. I am quite prepared to wait for the truth about quarks. I remain in a state of doubt and uncertainty awaiting future research and verification — and it may not come in my lifetime. On the other hand, I am unprepared to acknowledge that some genius out there in the Star Trek generation will discover the meaning of life — mine included.

Someone wrote to Kant after the publication of the *Critique of Practical Reason* to congratulate him on the "discovery of the moral law." The old philosopher wrote back expressing horror that he should have *discovered* the moral law. He might have offered a new *formula* for the moral law, but what had humankind been up to all those millennia waiting for Kant to discover morality? Kant's insight is correct, and one which ought to be acknowledged in the palace of intellect. Humankind will certainly wait on the patient investigations of science to reveal new truths. It will be and should be resistant to the notion that morality and the meaning of existence utterly await discovery.

The real issue for the contemporary university is whether it wants to pursue life wisdom at all. From the standpoint of the Cartesian self, the de-historicized mind of scientific investigation, there is no problem of life wisdom, because there is no life to be led. Years ago Jacques Maritain accused Descartes of "angelism": angels are pure intelligences without bodies and have no need of salvation. One can easily move from Descartes to Spinoza and dissolve the multiplicity of minds and selves into modes of eternal Substance. Whatever transcendent tranquillity this may yield, it hardly seems the answer to my particular life, which is cast aside as mere accident.

I can well imagine that the university could simply give over the search for life wisdom and productively pursue the advance of physics. In a sense, biblical religion might accept this stance, since in my construal religion is not a set of truths to be injected into the university; it is a life lived, it is a way of life, not a philosophy. The college is not the church — a vehicle of salvation; the church is not a college with some insight into science. Nevertheless, I continue to think that a Christian college makes sense because there is a reflexive moment from which the distinctions I have urged in this essay need to be articulated and defended to make way for revelation — or for revelation to make way for science. The claim that there is salvation, that the embodied life is not irrelevant, is a claim upon and against the human intellect which poses significant philosophical problems.

It is because the meaning of life cannot be something utterly surprising out there in the future, that the minute one introduces into the academy authored voices seeking the meaning of an embodied life, one begins to be obsessed with the problem of "the canon." A canon is the collection of voices with which the meaning of life has been uttered. Canon is not a very useful notion in science because the scientific "canon" lies in some far-off, verified future, not a revealed past. Because the meaning of life is not a radical discovery wholly out there in the future, one has to pay attention to history and tradition. Even those who reject the traditional canon will claim that there have been voices *already spoken* which at least adumbrate the meaning of life for women or blacks or whatever special history makes special claim on my existence. Christianity has a canon based on what it claims to be the unsurpassable word, the basic germ of the human story. Whether that is a claim to be accepted can only be assessed from a deep immersion in other claimants to canonic history.

If one takes the Hebrew Bible or the Christian testament as already authoritative, one must deal with three very significant qualifications: (1) the biblical canon is only the "germ"; (2) the germ is developed in innumerable biographies; (3) the development is in ongoing life, not art, science, and generality. Christianity as life is messy, confused, wasteful — but splendid — and in living we come to incarnate and understand the biblical "germ."

Let me end by applying these three qualifications to my own religious community of Roman Catholicism. In one sense the Catholics have it right in the emphasis on church and tradition over various reformist attempts to return to the supposed pure Christianity of the Gospels. The Gospels may contain the germ, an authoritative life, an unsurpassable word, but the "germ" is no more the whole Christian story than Henry James's germ constituted the written-out novel *The Spoils of Poynton.* What is written out in the subsequent history of the Christian community is as much an interpretation of the New Testament story as the story is an interpretation of subsequent history. There is, as Cardinal Newman said, a *development* of Christian doctrine.

Having noted that the Catholics have it right, let me say that they have manifestly not practiced their own best theory. While resisting the impossibility of fixing the story to the "pure" gospel of the early Christians, Catholic officials have been quite ready to fix the Christian story to Scholastic philosophy, the Council of Trent, or the latest *monitum* from Rome. Let me then end this lecture as any good Catholic would by giving advice to the pope — who, like any good pope, is not likely to pay much attention.

Since I started this talk by blaming the Jesuits, let me give them the final positive word. The advice comes from an old Spanish Jesuit as he is depicted in Robertson Davies's wonderful series of novels *The Deptford Trilogy.* It is a plea for the Holy Spirit — which is the ongoing life of the Pentecostal church. The conversation is between the old priest and the protagonist of the novel about the second coming. The priest speaks:

My idea is that when He comes again it will be to continue his ministry as an old man. I am an old man and my life has been spent as a soldier of Christ, and I tell you that the older I grow the less Christ's teaching says to me. I am sometimes very conscious that I

[189]

am following the path of a leader who died when He was less than half as old as I am now. I see and feel things that He never saw or felt. I know things that He seems never to have known. Everybody wants a Christ for himself and those who think like him. Very well, am I at fault for wanting a Christ who will show me how to be an old man? All Christ's teaching is put forward with the dogmatism, the certainty, the strength of youth: I need something that takes account of the accretion of experience, a sense of the paradox and ambiguity that comes with years! I think that after forty we should recognize Christ politely but turn for our comfort and guidance to God the Father, who knows the good and evil of life, and to the Holy Ghost, who possesses wisdom beyond that of the incarnated Christ. After all, we worship a Trinity, of which Christ is but one Person. I think that when He comes again it will be to declare the unity of the life of the flesh and the life of the spirit. And then perhaps we shall make some sense of this life of marvels, cruel circumstances, obscenities, and commonplaces. Who can tell? — we might even make it bearable for everybody.[6]

I suggest that our ancient biblical story qualifies by now to speak from the spirit of age: from the Hebrew Father who knows good and evil and the Christian Holy Spirit who knows what Jesus could not have known. But if biblical religion is to speak an authoritative word to the many voices clamoring to be heard on our campuses and across the regions of humankind, it will be because it contains not just the voice of Mosaic scribes or Paul of Tarsus, but the voices of rabbinic Judaism, the ecstatic moments of the Hasidic rebbes, of Thomas Aquinas and Dorothy Day, of Bonhoeffer and Hildegard — as well as many saints, heroes, and an innumerable host of us sinners. Perhaps in that way "we shall make some sense of this life of marvels, cruel circumstances, obscenities, and commonplaces. Who can tell? — we might even make it bearable for everybody."

6. Robertson Davies, *Fifth Business,* in *The Deptford Trilogy* (London: Penguin Books, 1983), p. 170.

BOBBY FONG

Afterword:
Turning Conflicts into Conversations

THE ANNOUNCED PURPOSE of the three-day conference on "Christianity
and Culture in the Crossfire" was to bring a distinguished group of
scholars and interested citizens together to reflect on how disputed
issues of relativism, feminism, cultural diversity, and postmodernism
bear on Christian commitment. It was proposed that the "culture wars"
have too often found writers on community, gender, and the social bases
of knowledge on one side, and Christians, as defenders of both deity
and the ideal of objective and impartial knowledge, on the other. It is
not surprising, given the thoughtfulness of our keynoters, whose
addresses constitute the essays in this collection, that the very polarities
and metaphor of this conference theme were de-constructed in the course
of the proceedings, which I review here in an order that helps point to
several common threads.

Martin Marty has asserted that it isn't a matter of two sides, but a
virtual universe of diversities that makes up the American cultural
fabric. We are not humans in general, citizens in general, cultured in
general, but locate ourselves in particular identities and loyalties. The
challenge of criss-crossing multicultures is to learn ways by which one
connects with the "other," to imagine life as it is lived by the "not-me's,"
and to engage in the political accommodations that make pluralistic
life possible.

Elizabeth Minnich has urged us to eschew the metaphor of war in favor of relationality, to encourage the silent and the silenced to find voice and to hear their stories. This also means refusing to settle for premature unity, the assumption that common ground is easily forged. Universals are too often overgeneralizations, based on false partialities, and we need to rightly esteem the particularities of experience as a way of moving from partiality to the task of forging bonds of community.

Jean Hampton, whose untimely death intervened between the conference and the publication of this collection, has urged us to engage in "productive" fighting, that is, reasoned disputation that respects the opponent. The object is not to win the fight, but to clarify issues and choices so that people can make informed choices of how to live. This involves entertaining the extent to which those with whom we most disagree may be right.

Miroslav Volf has invoked the figure of Jesus to remind us that connectedness and relationality cannot be fought for, are not the products of violence. Christ's kingdom is not forged by the powers of the world. Truth is not simply proclaimed, but lived, and the truthful life in Christ must include the willingness to embrace the "other," for it is those outside the gates to whom the good news was given and is good news.

So if there are no sides in the culture wars, and we must be conscientious objectors to the idea of wars and the weapons of the world, what alternative themes animated our deliberations? There are two, summed up in the words "community" and "conversation." Connectedness and relationality have to do with life in the *polis,* life together. And such bonds are forged by talk, by the sharing of stories.

Jack Neusner has called for reaffirmation of religion as encounter with God. Religious community is founded on the stories of such encounters, and although it is important to maintain the community, we must not forget that the community was made for God, not gods for the community. The holy texts of religious traditions remind us of the primacy of the encounter; their stories of meeting God should remind us of the possibility and duty of our own encounters, individually and corporately, with the divine.

Nick Wolterstorff has asserted in turn the importance of narrative identities in the academy. Interpretation and understanding depend not only on the object of study but also on the perspective brought by the scholar to the object. Thus our narrative identities may affect what we choose to study and what we deem important about what we find. Academic discourse has been enlarged, then, to include the life narratives of the citizens who constitute the academy.

Wayne Booth has used the example of deconstruction, as exemplified in the work of Jacques Derrida, to argue that postmodernism provides "a resurrection of humane rhetoric" that counters the sterility of positivist assumptions of what counts as human knowledge. Suspicious as religion and postmodern hermeneutics may be of each other, both acknowledge fundamental discontinuities in the world and in ourselves and offer narratives to contend with the brokenness of the human condition.

We move, then, from metaphors of conflict to metaphors of community, from the impasse of confrontation to the bridges of narrative. In listening to one another, and in honoring one another's stories, one another's particularities, we create a climate for civil discourse and civil life to which academics aspire, for which our society yearns, and to which the children of God are called.

Our hope in convening the conference was to encourage a conversation, peace negotiations in the culture wars. The presenters talked about affirming particularities by finding cross-cultural ways in which differences can be understood and accommodated. They acknowledged that talking across and about difference could be immensely frustrating and painful, that the probability of misunderstanding and misspeaking is rife, with those "mis"-ses maiming those we did not intend to hurt. Indeed, several presentations pointed out one way of knowing that had not been invited to the table. Peter Paris contended that "Western culture is not a necessary condition for the exercise of modern science and technology. Rather, the latter two transcend all cultural limitations and consequently are potentially available to all cultures." However, as Paula Brownlee has suggested, even with greater place given to scientists, we would still have difficulty understanding one another. We still need the development of a language of public discourse that transcends divisions both without and within the academy, for we are in effect still strangers to one another, riven by C. P. Snow's two cultures, by the burgeoning of particularities in postmodern concepts of the humanities, by the gap between academic and nonacademic culture, and by a corresponding abyss between sacred and secular sensibilities. That's a lot of bridging for language to do.

Yet we must begin. First, by being more aware of who has not been invited to the table. That, if anything, is one lesson of postmodern particularity. Second, by being ready for the pain and frustration of misspeaking. Words can wound, but bullets kill, and with Jean Hampton I have come to believe that fighting with words is preferable because it is not physically lethal, although words do leave emotional and spiritual scars, and sometimes it takes just as much courage to return to a conversation as it does to a battlefield, just as much discipline to be civil and respectful as it does to march in ranks under fire. Third and finally, I want to adapt Dennis O'Brien's image of the "shape-shifter." I would contend that both science and the postmodernist humanities are shape-shifters: science in its pace of change and post-modernism in its continual reconstitution of methods and identities.

In the Greek story of Proteus, Menelaus must embrace and hold the shape-shifter through all its manifestations before it yields to him its secrets of the future. In an eerily reminiscent scene in Genesis, Jacob wrestles all night with an angel of the Lord before it yields and blesses him. We believe in the fundamental value of the academy, and we believe also that education yields strength for living. It must, then, be worthwhile to wrestle with the shape-shifting particularities so well enunciated in the contributions to this collection, and the additional shape-shifters barely invited to the table. Excellent things are difficult to achieve, but being willing to shoulder the burden of difficulty is to pay due respect to that excellence.

And in faith, where knowledge fails, and tongues cease, there is still love. Love for our subjects, love for the human beings to which we must rightly, in the end, be devoted. I have referred to the language of science and the need for a language of public discourse; let me also invoke the language of love. Mark Schwehn made reference in his essay to the woman in the Gospel of Mark, "the first postmodern Christian," who spoke, finally, not in words, but in gesture. As we wrestle with angels and shape-shifters, let us remember that wrestling entails embracing the other, and an embrace can be an expression of love, especially where words fail. Love the Lord your God with all your heart, soul, strength, and mind, and love your neighbor as yourself. In this is all the wisdom of the law and the prophets. And so as we go into the world to serve God and our neighbor, let us remember, in the midst of the culture wars, that blessed are peacemakers, for they shall be called the children of God.

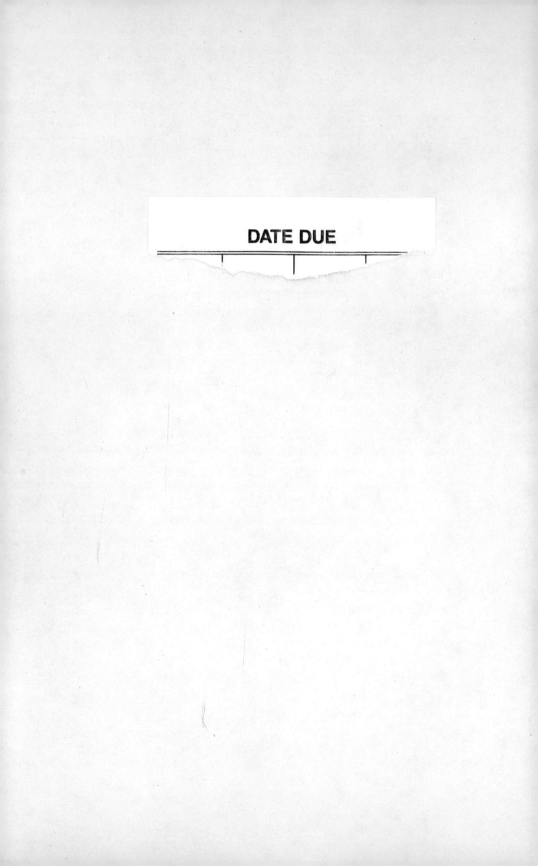

DATE DUE